WHY DO YOU NOT BELIEVE?

Why Do You Not Believe?

Rev. Andrew Murray

BAKER BOOK HOUSE
Grand Rapids, Michigan

Reprinted 1979 by
Baker Book House Company
from the edition issued by
Fleming H. Revell Company

ISBN: 0-8010-6090-7

PHOTOLITHOPRINTED BY CUSHING - MALLOY, INC.
ANN ARBOR, MICHIGAN, UNITED STATES OF AMERICA
1 9 7 9

To

Anxious Souls in my own Congregation,

and in

Every other where this Message is Read

with fervent prayers for

their salvation.

A. M.

TRANSLATOR'S NOTE

———◆———

In recently presenting the author's book on *The New Life* in an English dress, I remarked that it was specially adapted to those who had just come to the knowledge of the truth, and felt the want of guidance in the ways of the Lord. The present work is still more elementary. As its title implies, it is meant for those who have simply been aroused to the necessity of salvation, and who desire above all things to become Christians.

The method which the author adopts in dealing with these souls is seen at a glance to be entirely trustworthy. There are two classes of preachers that in our day claim to be evangelical. Some are so eager to make disciples that they do not hesitate to receive as such all who profess to acknowledge in any practical form the supremacy or authority of the Lord Jesus; others again act on the principle that the only way in which any-

one can become a genuine disciple is to exercise
a divinely-given faith in the once crucified but
now glorified Son of God—a faith that quickens
the soul, fills it with the Spirit of Christ, and so
unites it to Him for ever. It is to this latter
class that Mr. Murray belongs. The instrument-
ality for arriving at faith is the word.   To
hear the truth and not believe in Him of whom
it testifies is a position so unnatural and un-
reasonable that no pains should be spared to
dislodge the soul from it.   Hence it is that the
writer rings out so earnestly the keynote struck
by the Master in dealing with the Jews, "If
I speak the truth, why do ye not believe Me?"
(John viii. 46). Assured like Paul, as taught
by the Lord, that the only mode of receiving
forgiveness of sins and inheritance among them
that are sanctified, is "faith" in Christ (Acts
xxvi. 18), he concentrates the attention of the
anxious soul on the Saviour, on the one hand,
and on the necessity and power of faith in his
own heart, on the other. By this means he
expects that, under the working of the Spirit,
the soul will sooner or later be led to live the
life it lives in the flesh in faith, "the faith
which is in the Son of God, who loved me and
gave Himself up for me" (Gal. ii. 20).

That the little book will play a useful part in

our modern Evangelism, I cannot doubt; especially if its lessons are taken up and amplified by skilful teachers and class leaders. Those who remember the great influence wielded in their day by such books as Dr. Angell James' *Anxious Inquirer*, and Dr. H. Bonar's *God's Way of Peace*, will not be slow to expect that a large blessing will be vouchsafed to a similar help, in some respects more closely adapted to the wants of the present day. Already in South Africa it has had a wide welcome. In Holland, where I first saw it, it passed through six editions in a very short time. In Britain also, may it prove a messenger by which multitudes of the careless and indifferent adherents of the Church shall at once be awakened to the need of a vital bond betwixt Christ and their souls, and be led to fall back on that Spirit of faith by whom this need will be so richly supplied.

J. P. L.

ARBROATH,
January 1894.

" If I speak the truth, why do ye not believe Me ? "

CONTENTS

———◆———

INTRODUCTION

BELOVED friends, who are seeking the Lord, but have not yet found Him, it is for you that this little book has been written. When I recently spoke with you, in the course of my pastoral visitation, my soul was filled with deep sorrow over your condition. I still met with many who with manifest earnestness and spiritual desire were seeking salvation, some indeed for many years past, and who, notwithstanding, had not yet arrived at faith.

This ought not to remain so. It tends to the dishonour of our Lord. True religion is thereby brought into contempt, for the world is then right in concluding : the service of Jesus gives neither joy nor salvation. On young converts your influence is by no means helpful, for your example gives them absolutely no encouragement. In this way also, the congregation suffers loss, for instead of helping as joyfully active members to build it up, you are on the contrary serving to divide its energies, and you hinder its spiritual prosperity. To your minister you are often the cause of care and anxiety; you make him dispirited with the thought that the Word of God has so little influence with you. You spend your life in sorrow and gloom, and you place your souls in peril for eternity.

Beloved, your condition goes to my heart, and many a time I ask myself, What is really the cause of this unbelief? I know that there are some who cannot believe, because their heart is not right before God. The man who loves the world, and does not, with confession of his guilt, betake himself to Jesus with the prayer that he may be delivered from the love of the world, cannot, may not, believe. The man who still cleaves to this and that bosom sin, and, for instance, will not have done with deception, love of strife, pride, avarice, and such like iniquities, ought not to be surprised that he cannot believe. Jesus would ask him, "How can ye believe?" (John v. 44). It is an impossibility. But, beloved, we are persuaded better things of you. I write to you as those of whom I hope that it is in truth their earnest desire to find the Saviour, and of whom I really trust that they have truly declared before the Lord: Lord, Thou knowest all things, Thou knowest that I love Thee. And with my eye fixed on your condition, I ask myself, What can be the cause of it, and is there no means of delivering you out of it? *"Is there no balm in Gilead? Is there no physician there?"*

The cause cannot be that God has closed His dealings with you, and that it is no longer possible for you to believe. No: God commands you to believe. He desires this, and in His word has laid down before your faith promises for it to take up. And yet I fear that there are some among you who imagine that there is an appointment of God, against which you can do nothing, until God makes some alteration. With all earnestness, I entreat you to put these thoughts far from you. It is your own guilt that you do not believe, and indeed a heavy guilt, which you ought to confess with humility, and of which you should be ashamed. If you do not fully acknowledge this, I see no remedy for bringing you to faith, for this secret thought will make all your endeavours of no avail.

The cause of this unbelief of yours can just as little be that God has not given you power for faith. I know that this misunderstanding is prevailing with some of you. Because there are some Christians that have been brought to faith very suddenly and effectually, it is imagined that such a mode of conversion, if not the only one, is certainly at least the best. Secretly, therefore, some are waiting for a powerful impulse whereby they shall be as if driven to faith and brought to it at once. This thought also is a very dangerous hindrance in the way of faith. There are always two ways, along which one can attain to the enjoyment of abundance. To make the first plain by an example : one may become rich at once by an inheritance that one receives, or by this or that successful undertaking; but one can also attain to wealth by the more gradual and quiet method of faithful industry and economy, or by making a wise use of every opportunity of increasing one's resources. So, to use another illustration, one can have a large space filled with water by a plentiful shower of rain as well as by a watercourse from a clear fountain; by which latter method the thing is done more slowly. The first is the easier way, but it is also that which stands exposed to the most dangers the second is the longer and more troublesome way, but in some respects also the safer. The souls that find the heavenly treasure of the assurance of faith at once are to be accounted happy that the way for them has been so short; if others have to tread a more difficult path, they can nevertheless at least reach the goal. If they only move along the pathway of means with real desire, and with the positive conviction that they also can believe, they shall be brought to this point.

In connection with the two erroneous ideas just mentioned, stands what I have also just referred to, namely, the means of healing for your complaint, and therefore on this point, too, I shall say a few words.

You must acknowledge that it is the will of God that you should believe. "If I speak the truth, why do you not believe me?" (John viii. 46). This question of the Lord Jesus to the Jews, which He also puts to us, shows that unbelief must have a cause apart from Him. He spoke the truth with the aim and desire of awakening faith. You must further take into consideration that there is nothing for which you have to wait, before you begin to believe. You have to set yourselves forthwith in the way of the means, and with them you must be diligent; then you may hope for the blessing of the Spirit. On the Spirit you have not to wait, as if He had still first to come and were to make you by one token or another know that He was now ready, and that you could thus believe. No; He is promised to you. He has already often desired to work in your souls; and instead of your

having to wait for Him, before you begin to
believe, you have just to make haste to believe,
for the Spirit waits for you. You have already
kept Him waiting too long. Begin, therefore,
immediately without further delay. And if,
trusting in the promises of God, that the Spirit
is given to those who ask for Him, you are
diligent in learning to believe, you may also
certainly expect that He, the Spirit of grace,
will make you capable of faith. Wait not then,
and delay not under the impression that all is
not yet ready, or that it is not yet your duty
actually to believe. In this sense there is
nothing for which you have still to wait. No:
ask for the Spirit, expect His influence, be
diligent, and, although you do not then as yet
actually observe His workings, you may, nevertheless, reckon upon it that, even while you
may suppose yourselves to have been passed by,
the Spirit is already co-operating with your first
feeble endeavours.

You must pay special attention to what the
means for coming to faith is, and to what way it
has to be used. The means is the word: but
the main stress falls on the manner in which
the word is employed. When one searches it
merely in a general way, and reads it to get
knowledge and religious instruction, it operates

so strongly in the line of reflection and repentance that the anxious soul is often embarrassed by the influx of thought, and thus fails to attain his object in reading. It is my counsel, therefore, that you should read the Bible with a definite aim, namely, to find out what promises there are that you have to believe. It is my counsel that you should seek and come to know what promises there are that are available for you, in order that you may be occupied with them, and so take advantage of every expedient for receiving them in faith. Meditate upon them, learn them by heart, remain continuously absorbed with them, bow your knees before the Lord, and say to Him that you are resolved to believe them. Grudge not the time that this exercise costs you. Do not fancy that this business can be finished in ten minutes or so. The vast eternity is surely worth the striving of some hours. Take time thus to search the word with set purpose, with that one definite aim of arriving at faith. Ponder the word and pray for enlightening influences from above: such earnestness cannot remain unblessed.

There is still another remark to be made respecting the manner in which this means is to be used, namely, that the duty is to be done with faithfulness and perseverance. We all

know how great the power of habit is. By
continuous and intentional repetition a thing
that was at the outset strange and opposed to
our taste, becomes a second nature and thereby
easy and acceptable. In religion the laws of
human nature are not set aside; the Spirit is
indeed above them, but He still makes use of
them. So is it also with faith. The heart that
is habituated to distrust and doubt does not
arrive at the new, holy habit of faith without
the continual, often-repeated exercise of the act
of faith. The promise that found a slight
entrance to-day loses its influence in turn to-
morrow, just because the soul does not persevere
and has taken no pains to keep and confirm the
blessing received. Thus I have often observed
that, after a sermon or a conversation, a soul had
a little light but speedily again lost it. And
why? Because he did not recognise the importance and the necessity of his still keeping the
promises anew before him, to the end that the
old habit of unbelief might not again obtain the
upper hand. Therefore, beloved, be faithful, continue FROM DAY TO DAY, YES, AS MUCH AS YOU CAN,
occupied with the promises of God. The question
must be continually repeated, "What does God
require me to believe?" and in like manner, in
the face of whatever weakness, must the answer

be expressed at His feet: "Lord, I believe; I will believe."

To hold out a helpful hand to this perseverance, I have written for you this little book. It is offered to you with this urgent entreaty that for a month, day by day, you specially concentrate your attention on that faith to which God calls you. It was in the midst of prayer that these words were addressed to you: do you read them also with a praying heart. May it please the Lord to deliver you soon from the chains with which you to this day are still fettered. God grant it. Amen.

CHAPTER I

The Absolute Necessity of Faith

"He that believeth and is baptized shall be saved; but he that disbelieveth shall be condemned."—MARK xvi. 16.

HEAR this word of the Lord, all ye who have decided to seek your salvation.

He that believeth shall be saved; simple faith is enough: more God does not require. With less, however, He will not be content. Faith is the only way: there is no other way that leads to salvation. *He that disbelieveth shall be condemned.* Thus, alike on the right and the left hands, on the one side by the attractions and charms of His grace, on the other by the menace of His wrath, does God seek to impel us to faith in Christ as the one indispensable condition of salvation.

However much man may be opposed to this method of God, the time comes when the lost in hell no less than the saved in heaven shall justify God in this ordination of His. The whole universe shall acknowledge the equity of this sentence: *he that disbelieveth shall be condemned.* The gracious Lord had always met the sinner with the wonderful offer of having remitted all the offences he had committed, or what the law had still to demand—of having bestowed on him all that was necessary for an everlasting salvation. He required no worthiness or merit, but simply this, that man should accept what was offered to him, and believe what was said to him. And, in order to remove every impediment to faith out of the way, and win the heart, God ordained to be sent the glad tidings of salvation through His own Jesus Christ, who manifested Himself in the most loving and attractive form, and sealed His love with His own precious blood. He, then, that still does not believe—the whole creation must approve of the sentence—*he shall be condemned.* He has anew set the seal upon all his former sins, for he will not suffer himself to be redeemed from them. To his former sins, he has yet added this, the greatest of all, that he has affronted the authority of God, despised the love of God, lightly esteemed the Son of God, defied God's vengeance, and thrust away from him God's salvation. By unbelief he has shown his enmity against God and his rejection of God;

it cannot, it may not, be otherwise: *he that disbelieveth shall be condemned.*

Not less is the absolute necessity of faith confirmed by the contemplation of the other side: *he that believeth shall be saved.* Man has nothing, absolutely nothing, whereby on his part he can be in a position to contribute something to the attainment of salvation. And yet the Lord will do nothing but reign over a willing people. Man is no stone; on his own side, he must play his own part. It is faith that solves the difficult enigma that man who can do nothing should yet do something: faith which is manifested in the acknowledgment of poverty and misery, in the confession of inability and helplessness, in consent, submission, and surrender to that grace of God which is to be everything in us. More God could not require; less He may not require, for He will not inflict wrong on His own honour and the freedom of man. He requires faith: faith alone. What grace it is that thus bends to our weakness: *he that believeth shall be saved.*

Reader, behold, then, these two ways: make your choice. Pray, reason not any longer, nor ask the question if there be no other way; but, come, submit yourself to God and to the word of His grace: *he that believeth shall be saved.*

No longer yield to the secret thought, that something else may after all still be necessary. I am well aware that everlasting salvation appears to you to be too great a boon over against this meagre and paltry faith. It appears to you too hazardous for your sinfulness to venture so far merely upon faith; yet, see, it is God that has spoken: *only by faith.* He that possesses this faith, has all; for by it he has Christ. He that does not possess faith has nothing, although he should possess all besides. Faith is indispensable.

Anxious ones, hear it yet once again: "*he that believeth shall be saved; he that disbelieveth shall be condemned.*"

CHAPTER II

The Object of Faith

"**For she** said, If I but touch His garment**s** I shall
be made whole."—MARK v. 28.

*WHAT a glorious representation of the Lord
Jesus* does this woman in her simplicity
give to us. She regarded Him as so filled with
the divine power of life, as He in truth is, that
it flowed out on every one that only touched
Him in faith, and streamed over him. She felt
assured that even the slightest fellowship with
Him would be blessed, and that she would
experience the healing power of the life that
was in Him. Not for a moment did she have
any doubt of His power and still less of His
willingness. Had He not come for the sick?
Why should she still ask, as if she had no
claim? No: she knew the one truth just as
certainly as she knew the other—that in Him
there was healing. This healing is also for her.
She should doubt her right to make use of the
light of the sun, sooner than her right to Jesus.

She should fear whether it were indeed open to
her to take a draught of water from a rushing
river sooner than cherish the thought that there
was no health for her to be found with Jesus.

O that thou, doubting soul, wouldst think of
the Lord Jesus just as this woman thought of
Him. It is always the good pleasure of the
Father that in Him all fulness should dwell.
All the fulness of His love and His life has the
Father of set purpose made to dwell in Jesus,
the Son of Man, in order that it may be truly
visible and accessible to us. In Him dwells the
power of a new and holy life from the dead,
which he obtained by making atonement for our
sins. This life is mighty to impart health to
souls sick unto death, and this is for us sinful,
dead, condemned sinners. Pray, do understand
what the woman calls out to you; the blessing
and the approval of Jesus are always the seal of
the truth of her words. In Jesus is life, life
even for the most wretched.

*What a glorious representation is there here
also of true faith*, as the means of our partici-
pating in the fulness of Jesus. The woman
knows that she has no work to do; that she has
no great motion of strength to put forth; that
she has not to consider, as is the case in dealing
with other professors of the healing art, whether

she is really in a position to pay the fees that
will be demanded. No: she has merely to *touch*
Him, that is, she has merely to appropriate what
is prepared for her; the healing is there as soon
as she stretches out her hand to receive it.
Anxious soul, who hast already been so long
seeking to prepare and make yourself fit for the
great work of believing, let this poor woman
cure you of your error. In Jesus everything is
ready; you have merely to stretch out your
hand. O, do understand it. Here He stands
ready for your deliverance; He is also given to
you by the Father; only touch Him with the
firm conviction of the faith: *Jesus is for me;*
with the simple thought, I have a right to Him;
in Him there is deliverance for me also. Touch
Him, and, as truly as His name is Jesus, you
shall be delivered. This may not be immediately
felt by you; in that case just wait, hold on, say
from day to day: "If I touch Him, I shall be
made whole." The healing will be consciously
yours.

*And what a glorious representation is there
besides of the blessing which Jesus will give to
faith.* That the woman was healed was much
to begin with; but it speaks of yet richer
blessing that Jesus observed her, the poor
trembling believer who would fain have hid

herself for shame, even whilst others were seeking her in the crowd. He gives her the assurance of His good pleasure and His favour; He constrains her to confess Him openly. He praises her faith, and thus makes her an example and a blessing for thousands. O, all ye who are looking out and yearning for the salvation of the soul, pray learn to understand what is awaiting you with Jesus, what you may hope for from Him. It is not only forgiveness of sins and rescue from destruction that He will make you partakers of: the friendship and love of the Saviour shall also be your portion, and by these He will make you become a blessing to others.

Beloved, what more have you need of to make you say humbly and with faltering lips, after this woman, "*If I but touch His garments, I shall be made whole*"?

CHAPTER III

The Seed of Faith

" The seed is the word of God."—LUKE viii. 11.

VERY simply as well as strikingly is the word of God set forth to us in this parable. There lies the cold, dead earth, which of itself brings forth either nothing, or thorns and thistles. It has not the power to give man nutritive corn. When the husbandman, however, desires to have that corn, he takes good seed and commits it to the ground that had hitherto brought forth nothing but weeds. The soil receives it, and keeps it in the silent and dark secrecy of its bosom. Encouraged by the sunshine and moistened by the dew of heaven, it shoots there and grows up; and the cold dead earth by and by becomes the mother of a beautiful crop. The life was not in the earth, but in the seed; and yet the earth was just as indispensable as the living seed, before that these fair fruits could be reaped. Although the seed did not receive life from the earth, yet without the earth's having its share in the work, the seed could not yield its fruit. It must offer the seed the soil, in which the root can shoot; in its bosom must the seed still be kept until it be ready to make an appearance above ground.

A glorious and instructive picture is this of the new life of grace. Like the seed, the word has a divine power of life. Like the earth, the heart is in itself lifeless, unfruitful of itself in what is good. Like the seed in the earth, the word is strewn in the heart and committed to it, simply to be received and kept there. The living power that God has lodged in the seed is the security that the ground, although in and of itself wholly incapable of bringing forth anything but weeds, will be changed into a fruitful field. Thus, however helpless you may feel yourselves to be, shall the living seed of God's word send forth its roots in your heart, and sprouting upwards bring forth fruit. Sinner, yearning for salvation, you have only to acknowledge that a living power is presented to you in every word of God. With that confidence must you keep it in your heart, and the certainty of fruit depends not on any ability of *yours*, but on the faithfulness of God. Only endeavour by prayerful consideration and faithful keeping of God's word, to prepare a place for it in your heart.

Mourn no longer, then, that your heart is so hard and so full of weeds, but rather understand what you see every day, that by the keeping of the seed the dead earth is transformed into a fruitful field. Faith is not a thing that is present in you before you receive the word, or with which you must meet the word. No! *there is life in the word, and it is by the word that faith is first awakened.*

Meanwhile, forget not that there are many kinds of seed, and that every kind bears fruit according to its nature. A child of God, for example, longs for comfort in adversity; he chooses one of the promises of God to His people, sows it in his heart, and keeps it; the desired fruit is the comfort of God. As those who are troubled about your sins, you have need of the promises of God's grace in relation to the ungodly. Seek for seed according to your need. "The Lord is gracious and full of compassion"; "He will abundantly pardon"; "Him that cometh unto Me I will in no wise cast out"; Christ died for the ungodly."[1] That is the kind of seed you must use. Every one of these words is a heavenly grain of seed

[1] Ps. iii. 4 ; Isa. lv. 7 ; John vi. 37 ; Rom. v. 6.

containing power for eternal life. One of them is sufficient to bring forth, when it shoots up, the fruits of faith and peace and life. Let one of them be faithfully kept in the heart, and it cannot but be that faith shall be born of it. In the seed is life: the seed of God's word has a divine power of life. O, take, then, the heavenly seed, lay it up in your heart, and keep it there. Although you do not actually feel that you believe, resolve at least to hold fast by the thought: "It is the living word of God. God will give the increase in His own time." The seed needs time for development. It must be kept a long time quietly beneath the ground: one day it certainly comes up. Day by day continue absorbed in heart with the word of promise and of grace. The true God and His living word are the guarantees that your experience also shall be: "*Faith cometh by the word of God.*"

CHAPTER IV

The Language of Faith

"With Thee is forgiveness."—PSALM cxxx. 4.

HERE is one of those heavenly grains of seed that have only to be received and kept in the heart to become living, and to bring forth faith, peace, and blessing. Let me have the privilege of commending it to you this morning, anxious soul.

It is such a *simple* word : every one can understand it. Every one knows what is meant when an earthly father forgives his child. He answers him that he will no longer remember his sins, will not impute the evil experienced, and will not punish him. He will deal with the child as if he had done no harm. In like manner the guilty and consciously-condemned soul looks to God on high, and says : "Lord, with Thee there is forgiveness. My guilt is heavy, I have deserved Thy severest punishment ; but with Thee is forgiveness. Of free grace Thou hast promised to acquit the guilty of everything, and not to impute his sins to him." This is the simple, and at the same time the only way along which one exposed to the curse, who can do or bring nothing, can be saved. Altogether freely and for nothing, without the least worthiness or merit on his part, he receives the divine acquittal from all his guilt.

Is it not also a *glorious* word? Should not every one desire this boon? For a soul that, with David in this psalm, has to cry "out of the depths": "If Thou, Lord, shouldest mark iniquities, O Lord, who shall stand?" it is glorious to be able to look up to God with the assurance: All these sins will God blot out and bring to nought. Yes: very blessed it is to be able to look up to God out of the distress and anxiety with which the soul has felt its heavy guilt and deep misery, and to say: "With Thee is forgiveness; the Lord looks upon me in grace, His anger is turned away from me, and He comforts me." What a blessed peace, what a heavenly joy then falls on the heart. O, it is glorious, in the face of all conviction of sin and experience of misery, in the face of every thought of death and judgment, to be able to say: "With Thee is forgiveness." Who would not desire it?

It is also such a *sure* word. Every one may

believe it. The whole Bible announces it. Jesus
came from heaven to obtain and to seal it for us.
His blood is the pledge of it. Thousands of the
greatest sinners can support the truth of the cry:
"*With God there is forgiveness.*" All heaven
confirms it. Eternity shall re-echo: "*With God
is forgiveness.*" It is sure. The certitude of it
depends not on your faith. Whether you believe
it or not, whether you despise it or not, "With
God is forgiveness." As truly as He is God, is
He a God of forgiveness, a God who abundantly
pardons. As certain as you are that He is God,
may you be certain that there is forgiveness
with Him. Before you believe it, it is truth,
and you may rest your soul and safely commit
yourself to God upon it. You shall experience
it: with God is *sure* forgiveness.

Further, it is such a *powerful* word. Every
one can receive blessing from it. Although you
have as yet no faith, take this word as a living
seed into your heart, and it will awaken faith.
Although you dare not as yet call God your
Father, lay up this word in your heart, give it
a place there, think over it, and say in spoken
words before your God: "*Lord, with Thee there
is forgiveness.*" This word is living and powerful; it will cause hope to rise in your soul. It
will inspire you with new thoughts about God,

it will instil into you confidence and boldness before Him. Insensibly you will get up to saying: "With Thee there is forgiveness *also for me.*" It will thus awaken the fear and love of God in your soul. It will bind you to Jesus, it will impel you to dedicate yourself wholly to Him. O soul, mourn no longer over your weakness. Receive this word; it is "living and powerful." Go with it trustfully to your knees, and, although it should be the thousandth time, use it as the language of your heart to God: "*Lord, with Thee there is forgiveness.*" This word will work mightily, and faith and peace and love shall be its fruits.

Beloved, I offer to you this word of God. God gives you freedom to use this word with Him; God commands you to think thus of Him. True, your heart says, "I do not know whether there is forgiveness with God"; but come, let these perverse thoughts of yours go and give room for *God's* thoughts in your soul. Let it stand fast with you: "*With God is forgiveness,*" and you shall speedily be able to add: *also for me.* And so you shall soon learn to sing: "Bless the Lord, O my soul, who forgiveth all thine iniquities."

CHAPTER V

Tbe Beginning of Faith

" **Yea**, Lord, I have believed that Thou **art the** Christ, the Son of God."—JOHN xi. 27.

THE Lord had said to Martha: "I am the resurrection and the life: he that believeth on Me, though he die, yet shall he live"; and after that He had put to her the question, "Believest thou this?" What answer was she to give? The thought that her brother was to be raised again was still too high and wonderful for her. And yet she was conscious that she believed in Jesus, and did not doubt Him or His word. What reply was she to make? With childlike simplicity and sincerity she says: "I have believed that Thou **art the** Christ: I do not indeed know aright what I believe concerning the resurrection of my brother. It is to me, as if I cannot understand, cannot conceive it; but this I know, I have believed **and** still believe in Thee, as the Son of the living God. Thee, Thy birth, Thy power, Thy love, I doubt not."

How instructive is this picture of Martha's faith. How frequently it happens that when the word of the Lord comes to a soul with the promise of forgiveness and reception into childship with God, and the question is put, "Believest thou this?" that the discouraged soul falls a-sighing and answers, "Ah! no: this I cannot yet believe"; and thereafter he proceeds to condemn himself—a thing that profits nothing, instead of acting as Martha did. She did not yet believe *everything*, but what she believed that she spoke out before the Lord. She believed in Him as the Son of the living God: this was the principal thing, and would prove the source of greater faith. In connection with what she did believe, she was diligent in prayer; by this means her faith would be strengthened and become capable of receiving yet more and more.

Follow that example, O thou of little faith. When you are asked: Do you believe that your sins are forgiven, that you are a child of God, that everlasting salvation is yours? you are perhaps afraid to answer, "Yes." You see others who can say so. You read in God's word that the Lord will give His grace, that you may be

enabled to say so. But *you* cannot say so, and
you do not know how *you* shall ever come to the
point of daring to say so. Soul, learn the way
from Martha. Do not continue sitting down
there, mourning over your unbelief, but go to
Jesus with that which you *know* that *you* do
believe. This at least you know that, although
you cannot yet say, He is *my* Saviour, your
whole soul believes that He was sent by God to
be a Saviour, and that He has proved Himself
to be a Saviour for others. Well, then, go with
this confession to Jesus, utter it before Him in
prayer, look to Him and adore Him as the
Saviour of the world. Speak out what you do
believe, and by this means will faith in your
heart be confirmed and increased. Say: "Lord
Jesus, how unbelieving I am; this, however, I
do believe that Thou art the Saviour, full of
love and grace, and mighty to redeem." Forget yourselves and worship Jesus, although you
dare not as yet say, that He is yours. In the
midst of those exercises your faith will increase,
and by and by you will insensibly come to the
confidence that He is also *yours.* Only persevere: so long as you cannot yet say, "He is
mine and I am His," let your soul be found, this
and every day, in the ceaseless adoring confession: "Yea, Lord: this I believe, that Thou

art the Christ, the Son of the living God."   He will speedily confirm to you that word of truth : "Thou hast been faithful over a few things, I will set thee over many things ; enter thou into the joy of thy Lord " (Matt. xxv. 21).   You will speedily learn to believe, and then, like Martha, **you shall** also **see the** glory of God.

CHAPTER VI

The Spirit of Faith

"But having the same Spirit of faith . . . we also believe."—2 COR. iv. 13.

FOR the hundred times that in the word of God we are exhorted to faith, or that faith is spoken of as an act of man, it is but in some few instances that it is expressly said that faith is the work of the Spirit. And thus, when we insist on faith as a work in which man must be active and in which he must trustfully and perseveringly use means, it may sometimes appear as if we forget who the Author of faith is. This, however, is by no means the case. We believe that those who feel most deeply the truth about the complete dependence of man on the Spirit, as the Spirit of faith, will also be the most eager to fall in with the exhortation addressed to man. He who knows that there is a Spirit to actuate to faith knows also that man may, with spirit and hope, strive to exercise faith.

The right understanding of this truth is, for anxious souls, of great importance. They must especially know that when they wait for the influence of the Spirit to carry them on to faith, they must not expect that this influence shall be unveiled to them in a conscious and sensible manner. The beginnings of life are hid in darkness: the first workings of the Spirit are not known or observed. The soul must work on, although it be not conscious that the Spirit is in it: it must as readily in the dark as in the day, and that too in its own strength, obey and strive to believe; it must hold fast the word in confidence that the Spirit will, through the word, work in it, expecting that sooner or later the Spirit will be recognised as the power that has put it in a position to believe. That faith will then be to it the first sure token that it has the Spirit. He is always the Spirit of *faith*. Faith is his internal manifestation, the form in which He reveals Himself, and by which He becomes known. It cannot be, " If I once have the Spirit then I believe," but, " when I believe, then I know that the Spirit has wrought this result in me."

In this way the right desire of the soul to know that it has *the Spirit* of faith may be fully gratified. It will learn that there is something more in it than its mere faith, that faitn is not its own work : it will learn that the divine Creator of the new life is in it. According as the trustful soul is in itself un-reservedly surrendered to live through faith, shall the Spirit witness with its spirit which was active in faith, according to the word of God, that after we believe we are sealed with the Spirit : "*Ye know Him*, for He abideth with you and shall be in you" (John xiv. 17). By His divine, indwelling power, he always stirs up the soul more and more to faith, carrying it into all the riches of the promises of God, and giving it confidence to appropriate every blessing to itself. And thus the one influence always operates upon the other ; the more fully the soul believes, the more clear becomes the revela-tion of the Spirit ; the more fully the Spirit works in it, the more does the soul grow in the life of faith and confidence. And thus at length, but not by the way which most of us had pictured for ourselves, we come to the experience of the blessedness of which we are speaking, namely, of having the Spirit of faith.

Seeker of salvation, why do you not believe ? The Spirit of God is a Spirit of faith. It is the Spirit of God that has broken your slumber and made you anxious to believe. It is the

Spirit who will help you in the conflict for faith, in which you think that you are abandoned by Him. He is given in answer to prayer. Let the thought encourage you, that where there is a soul desirous of salvation the Spirit will certainly work faith in it. At the outset you are not yet in a position to recognise His working. You are not yet accustomed to His ways; His tokens are still unknown to you. Hidden, but really existing, He is at hand to help you, if you but pray for Him and do your work, relying upon His operation. In this exercise and conflict of prayer, and in the desire to believe, it is He that all unconsciously draws on and strengthens the soul. Believe, for the Spirit will give faith within you. Work, "for it is God that worketh in you."

And, when you have believed and have become known to Him as the Spirit of faith— O, be thou only faithful to Him. Yield yourself wholly to Him; set your heart entirely open for Him; through Him, let there be a progress "from faith to faith," until, with full certitude, you are able to witness: "We have the same Spirit of faith, therefore we also believe."

CHAPTER VII

The Repentance of Faith

'Repent ye, and believe in the gospel."—MARK i. 15.

THIS beginning of the preaching of the Lord
Jesus contains the summary of the will
of God for our salvation. Repent ye and believe.
What God hath joined together, let not man
put asunder. Without repentance no real faith,
without faith no true repentance.

Without repentance no real faith. The entire
design of God in the mission of Christ, the
great aim for which the salvation of faith has
been given to us, is to win the heart back from
sin, and to make it free from sin. A real desire
for this salvation can thus never arise in the
heart that is not also prepared to be loosed from
sin, and to abandon it. Faith is a surrender of
the soul to God: this is an impossibility where
it still continues to give itself to sin. Faith is
an appropriation and a reception into the heart
of the grace of God: it is an absurdity to
suppose that this should take place without a

contemporaneous repentance, an abandonment
and casting out of sin.

Without faith also no true repentance. Repentance is not only a turning away from sin,
which of itself would tend to self-righteousness,
but a turning back to God, and this can take
place only through faith. Repentance is not a
work of one's own power, but a consenting, a
co-operation with God's plan, in God's strength,
a trustful surrender to the redeeming grace of
God. And this can be done only through faith.
Repentance is not an actual victory over sin,
but the soul has to bring every sin to the feet
of the Lord Jesus, the great victor over sin,
that He may take it away; and this cannot
find place, except by the faith which has acknowledged that He is faithful to forgive sin,
and to cleanse from all unrighteousness.

Thus the power of repentance is faith: for
the more we trust that Jesus makes us free
from sin, the stronger are we to turn away from
it. And the power of faith, on the other hand,
is also repentance: for the more eager to become
freed from sin it causes us to be, the more are
we shut up to faith. "Repent ye and believe":
he that observes and holds fast both shall be
saved.

Nor is it only at the beginning of the way,

but on to the very end that these two must accompany one another. No sooner is faith cultivated in a one-sided fashion, without a growing conscientiousness in the casting off of little sins, and the sanctification of the whole heart and walk, than it becomes a work merely of the understanding or the feeling. And as soon as continued repentance occupies itself with the furtherance of sanctification, without daily holding fast and increasing a living faith by the promise of God's grace, such a repentance will also lose its worth.

"Repent ye and believe." See here what Jesus calls us to. Every wish and endeavour after repentance, every remembrance of the sin which is in you, and of which you would be free, must be a summons to faith in that Jesus who is exalted to bestow repentance. Combat every sin, and make renunciation of it at His feet with faith fixed on Him. And let every thought of faith on the other hand be an encouragement to fight more bravely against sin, until at length your whole soul shall be filled with the faith of which it is written: "This is the victory that overcometh the world, even your faith." So shall repentance and faith in due time become entirely one, and the out-going of the soul to Jesus shall be a departure from sin: the enjoyment by faith of the light of His love, shall of itself drive away the darkness. Then shall believing and working no longer be considered as antagonistic, but the soul shall know that a continually renewed faith is the fruit of sanctification, for it carries it on in the strength of Jesus, and continued repentance then gives to faith courage to per severe, experience which it can plead, and the certitude of a full assurance.

Soul, why do you not believe? O, pray let it not be because you will not repent. It should not be that you are not willing to make a renunciation of sin. And let it not be that you would first repent and then later on believe. No: let both go together from this moment onwards: "Repent ye and believe."

CHAPTER VIII

The Humility of Faith

"Lord, I am not worthy that Thou shouldest come under my roof: but only say the word, and my servant shall be healed."—MATT. viii. 8.

THE faith of which these words are the utterance was so great that the Lord wondered at it, and exclaimed: "I have not found so great faith, no not in Israel." It may be of service to those who desire to come to faith, or who long for a stronger faith than they have hitherto had, to examine carefully the faith of the centurion, and to observe the soil in which that great faith struck its roots. The soil is—deep humility. This man who, although he belonged to the Gentiles, was praised by the Jewish elders as worthy of the Lord's favour, and whose faith surpassed all that the Lord had found in Israel,—this eminent man is the only one of whom we read, during Jesus' sojourn on earth, that he did not consider himself worthy

that Jesus should enter his house. Wonderful
humility in such a hero of faith. We learn
from this the most momentous lesson—that deep
humility and strong faith are knit to one another
by the closest bonds.

Out of humility springs faith. Then first,
when the soul fully acknowledges that it has
nothing, and is also content to receive favour as
one that possesses nothing, does it cast itself on
the free grace of God, and receive it as one
that believeth. In the acknowledgment of its
nothingness, it does not dare to contradict God
with its thoughts of unworthiness, with its desire
still further to bring this or that to perfection.
It feels that, since it has pleased such a great
God to say that He is prepared to show compassion to the poorest and most wretched, then
nothing becomes it better than to be silent and
suffer Him to manifest His love. It knows,
moreover, that it is so deeply corrupt that it
can never of itself become better, and on this
account its faith is just the best proof of its
humility : it is from the recognition of its utter
helplessness, from its knowledge of the fact that
it can never become better, that it casts itself on
the will of God. This is an entirely different
state of mind from that of all such as imagine
that humility comes out in not believing ; as if

there could be humility in waiting till something
has been found in us that could make us more
acceptable to the Lord than we really are; as if
there could be humility in giving no obedience
to the command of God actually to believe.
Nay, verily. And just as perverse is the idea
that faith will at any later period lead to pride.
No: faith, as it springs from humility, will in
turn only increase humility. It was because
the centurion by faith recognised Jesus as
wielding over nature a power which could not
by any circumstance be prevented from healing
the sick by His mere word, that he felt himself
to be unworthy of having him in his house.
And thus will it always be. The more glorious
the revelation and experience of the Lord's
greatness and goodness which faith enjoys, the
more deeply does it sink in self-abasement and
in lowly acknowledgment of the condescension
by which such a God unveils Himself to such a
sinner. And thus it always continues to be:
the deeper humility the more faith, and again,
the stronger faith the deeper humility. May
the Lord teach us these truths—that there is
no stronger proof of humility, and also no better
means of increasing it, than just faith; and
that, whether we feel ourselves deeply humbled
or still desire to come to a deeper humility

the one as well as the other should only shut us up to faith.

And now, soul, why do you not believe? Are you still too unworthy? You dare not say so. The deeper your humility, the stronger your reason and right for believing. Are you still too proud? Ah, let it not be longer so. Only bring yourself to the acknowledgment of your entire weakness, and confess that you are wholly lost: in the depths of your wretchedness, you will see that there is no other remedy than to let the Lord help you, and to commit yourself trustfully to the word of His grace.

CHAPTER IX

The Finding of Faith

"Seek, and ye shall find."—LUKE xi. 9.

THIS word is a promise of Jesus, and on this account sure and certain. His truth and faithfulness are like His love to sinners, the pledge that every one who truly seeks shall certainly find. And yet there are so many that apparently seek sincerely and earnestly, and yet complain that they do not find. Whence arises this failure? Amongst other reasons, a principal one is that they do not know what finding is. They have a wrong idea of this finding; so that they have probably found, and yet continue seeking. And this arises chiefly from the fact of their not understanding that not only seeking and praying, but also finding must take place *by faith*.

To use an illustration: I have a heavy debt, and must go to prison, because I cannot pay it. I *seek* for a surety, but can nowhere find one. Then I receive a letter from a friend who has heard of my misfortune, telling me that he

will become my surety: he will come at the
first opportunity to release me. Shall I then
not say that I have *found* a surety? And that
not otherwise than by faith. I have not yet
spoken to the man, I have not yet received the
money, and yet out of trust in his letter, and
because I place reliance on his word, I still say:
I have found a surety. It might possibly happen
that experience here would be in conflict with
faith. Perchance I might be taken to prison on
account of my debt, and my actual experience
at that time, when I looked round on the
gloomy abode, might possibly say, "I have no
surety"; but faith would still say, "I have
found a surety; I know my friend will certainly
come. I have only to wait a little, when he
will appear for my release." The real experience then comes later—after the finding.

Not otherwise is it with the finding of the
Lord Jesus. The awakened sinner seeks all
round for a surety to meet his debt, to deliver
his soul, but nowhere finds one. Then comes to
him the word of God, with the message:
"Christ is a propitiation for the sin of the
whole world." The soul has only to receive
that word, and then by faith it has found a
Redeemer. And according as it occupies itself
with that word, so as to be persuaded that the

message is also for it, the more does it become
strengthened in the conviction: "The Redeemer
is also for me—God has said it"; until at last it
learns to say with gladness: "I have found the
Saviour." Mark it well, all this takes place
simply and only by faith in the word. It may
be that the soul's experience is still in conflict
with this confession. It often feels itself very
sinful, corrupt, perverted from God, as if it were
in a gloomy dungeon, and it asks: "If it be
true that I have found the Saviour, why is it
thus with me?" But it remembers that the
finding of the Redeemer precedes the real experience of redemption. It comforts itself with the
thought that the Lord is honoured by the faith
which holds fast His word as truth, and that it
is by trial that faith becomes prepared alike to
contemplate and to enjoy. First finding, receiving in faith; then later, actual experience.

Seeking soul, Jesus is to be found. He is
not far from you, so that you must still for a
long time seek Him, but very near. For He
seeks you. Only believe this, hem yourself
round with this: "Jesus seeks me, and is bent
on having me." Let the word of God's grace
fill your heart, and out of the word you will
speedily say in faith: "I have found Him whom
my soul desireth, Jesus, the Saviour of sinners."

CHAPTER X

The Simplicity of Faith

"The word is nigh thee, in thy mouth, and in thy heart."—ROM. x. 8.

THE righteousness which is of faith saith thus: "Say not in thine heart, Who shall ascend into heaven? (that is, to bring Christ down:) or, Who shall descend into the abyss? (that is, to bring Christ up from the dead.) But what saith it? The word is nigh thee, in thy mouth, and in thy heart: that is, the word of faith, which we preach." Thus does Paul describe the simplicity of faith and of the salvation which is obtained by it. Not in the height above, not in the depth below, not far off and to be sought for with great trouble: for the word is nigh thee, in thy mouth and in thy heart. That is to say, if you simply confess with the mouth the Lord Jesus, and believe in your heart, you shall be saved.

O that souls would give heed to such words of God, and understand that it is the truth, what God says: "Hearken unto me, ye stout-hearted, that are far from righteousness: I bring near my righteousness: it shall not be far off" (Isa. xlvi. 13). We are far from God, and yet we have no long road to traverse in seeking God. For such a task we are too weak and too blind. In sheer compassion He brings his salvation right up to us, yea, very nigh. Not in the height and not in the depth, but in our own inmost spirit He manifests His salvation. In our mouth and in our heart does He give it, for in the preaching of the word of faith Christ abides and He comes to us. And yet so many will always go about seeking it, as if it were afar off. How is it that they sigh over the thought of the majesty and the holiness of God and the impossibility of climbing up to Him to bring thence a Saviour for themselves? Or how is it that they speak of the Lord Christ, as if He were still dead (although He did indeed die for our sins), and did not now live to save them? Ah, no: that was the righteousness, which was of the law, and which prescribed that man must do something before he can live. But the message of the Gospel is: "Receive with meekness the im-planted word, which is able to save your souls" (James i. 21). Helpless and wretched,

man has only to be silent and to receive : God
brings the blessing nigh.

The word is nigh thee, in thy mouth and in
thy heart. You mourn that it is still not in
your heart. You are afraid to take it simply in
your mouth ; but, soul, observe how gracious God
is. He will make the confession of the mouth for
you the way and the means to the faith of the
heart. How often in the things of this world
do we teach our little children to utter words
which they do not yet fully understand, in the
sure confidence that the thoughts and feelings
expressed in them will be gradually imprinted on
their hearts. How constantly do we see that idle
and sinful words, which at the outset are uttered
carelessly, become forthwith rooted in the heart
of the speaker, and bear their own fruits. And
what do we not observe in prayer ? That the
soul which is ever and anon uttering, for example, the words, " Thy will be done," although
the heart does not as yet fully assent to them,
shall at last, by means of the very use of the
expression, submit to the casting out of the
unwilling and antagonistic disposition. Would
that we dealt not otherwise with the salvation
which is by faith. Take the word in your
mouth, humbly and earnestly. *Say the words
of grace after the Lord God,* as if you heard

Him addressing them to you. Yield not to the unbelief of the heart: combat and overcome it by attaching yourself to the Lord with the mouth: the consent of the heart will surely be won. Yea, do this now, by continually thinking over and speaking what the Lord God has said to you: "The word is nigh." Confess with the mouth, with longing and with prayer, in order that it may at length come to the faith of the heart, that Jesus is your choice and your Lord: the Spirit of God will work with the word, and you shall be able to believe with your heart. The word is nigh thee, in thy mouth and then also in your heart.

CHAPTER XI

The Sincerity of Faith

"**I believe;** help Thou mine unbelief."—MARK ix. 24.

THE word of God attaches great value to
sincerity. It is on this account that the
desire of many to be sincere in their faith is
justifiable. And for the fear and disquietude
which arise from this desire they have also well-
founded reasons, in the consistent testimony of
the word of God as well as in experience.
"The heart is deceitful above all things, and it
is desperately sick: who can know it?" (Jer.
xvii. 9).

Frequently, however, there are great mistakes
made, alike with respect to what true sincerity
is and the means by which it is obtained and
increased. As to the first of these points—what
true sincerity is—many think that sincerity
consists in a distinct feeling that they have
surrendered themselves to the Lord with a strong
faith and a fervent love. This is by no means
what the word of God intends by sincerity.

Sincerity is that attitude of the soul, in virtue of which we *present ourselves to the Lord just as we are*, neither better nor worse.   A man is insincere who makes himself out to be other than he really is or feels.   It is on this account that the words of the father of the possessed child, quoted above, are such a glorious example of sincerity. He wished to believe, but felt unbelief still too strong within him.   What, then, shall be done? He presents himself to the Lord just as he is. He knows that his desire is to trust in Jesus ; but he does not know whether there be more unbelief than faith in his heart.   What shall he do?   Shall he mourn over the unbelief that is still in him?   Or shall he just wait on till he feels that he has believed well and fully?   No : not one of these things ; for they will afford him no help.   Just as he is, he goes to Jesus, and with childlike sincerity and simplicity he pours out his heart before Him : " Lord, I believe : but, alas, there is still too much unbelief—come, to the help of my distrustfulness."

And this teaches us further what is the only means of being delivered from insincerity.   The father felt that there was still in him an element that was waiting to believe, but *he goes with it to Jesus*.   He makes it known to Him in the expectation that, in spite of his distrust, He will have mercy upon him and rescue him from it. How utterly different is this conduct from that of so many seeking souls. How often they continue year after year mourning over insincerity, longing for sincerity, and yet they make no progress. Ask them if it be not true that they make no advance but rather go on in their misery. And they know not, and they hearken not, when it is said to them that this is genuine sincerity—to present ourselves just as we are, with all our unbelief. They ought to know that this is the only way to healing; to give ourselves to the Saviour, with the little beginnings of good,—although they are but a desire to believe,—and that, too, in spite of a great preponderance of double-heartedness and worldlymindedness and unbelief. Yes: to mourn our unbelief, in dealing actually with Jesus—that is true sincerity.

Poor soul, who hast so long remained apart from the Lord from dread of being insincere, and hast thereby grieved both the Lord and thyself, even although thou shouldest feel that of the hundred elements in you there are ninety and nine of unbelief, and only one of feeble desire to believe, *go with it to Jesus: that is sincerity*. Continue every day also to pour out your heart before the Lord: fight the good fight against remaining insincerity and distrust at Jesus' feet. That is the only place where you can overcome. " Lord, I believe ; I will believe as well as I can ; I do so. I believe at last, that Thou art Jesus, the Helper of the wretched ; come to the help of my distrustfulness." As you thus pray and strive every day, you will soon obtain the victory and the blessing. As for him who does not thus pray, he may be sure at least of this, that, so long as he remains apart from Jesus, no more sincerity shall come. No : sincerity is the outpouring of the heart before the Lord, and is nowhere obtained but in inter-course with Him and through His friendly grace.

CHAPTER XII

The Penitence of Faith

" Depart from me ; for I am a sinful man, O Lord."
—LUKE v. 8. *Chapter 5*

THE Saviour had unveiled His glory to Peter. He had wonderfully blessed His work of faith, "At Thy word I will let down the net," and at the same time made Himself known as the mighty Ruler over nature, the beneficent Friend of His disciples. Of all this grace, the fruit and the result was that Peter cast Himself before the Lord with the prayer : "Depart from me ; for I am a sinful man." The glory of the Lord appeared to him so clearly in that light of faith, and his own sinfulness became to him so manifest, that out of dread and self - abasement he uttered this cry : a clear proof that true faith has as its fruit a deeper humiliation for sin and knowledge of it, sincere and inward penitence.

And this lesson is of great importance for many who are in the way of faith. They think

that they cannot be believing, because they are
not yet deeply enough convinced of sin. And
they do not observe that this word has not
yet defined how deeply one must feel sin before
one may come to Jesus: it has fixed no measure.
The first sense of need must bring us to Him.
They do not understand that this remaining
apart from Jesus is just the way to make their
sense of sin less, and, what is especially of
importance, that, on the other hand, an incipient
faith may become the means of increasing this
sense of sin. Always the closer to the light,
the more visible the impurity; the nearer to
the Holy One, the stronger the sense of unworthiness; the more blessed with grace, the
deeper the conviction of sin.

As with Peter, so with all believers. The
hour of the revelation of Jesus' grace and love
are the times of the deepest abasement. And
these times are for the most part not at the
beginning, but in the later progress of the life
of faith. Consider the case of Peter: he has
to attain his true knowledge of sin at his denial
of the Lord, well-nigh three years after he had
already said: "We have believed and known
that Thou art the Christ." Think also of
Jacob: how the Lord made with him at Bethel
the covenant of His grace, and yet first brought

him to the recognition of his sinfulness twenty
years later, in the crisis of the wrestling by
night, in which the Lord came to meet him as
an antagonist, to break down the old nature
and the power of the flesh. Think also of
David and the glorious experiences of God's
help and friendship which he as a youth tasted
when he was a shepherd and fought against
Goliath : it was much later in life that he had
to enter into the path of suffering, ere he could
see sin unveiled. And so there are still ever
so many, in whose case it is manifest that the
Lord first leads their souls to faith, and then
later on, through faith, to the full knowledge of
sin, to genuine penitence.

Accordingly, let the soul who desires to
become more humble and to turn back to God
as one that is guilty understand that doubt
and unbelief will not help him in this but
rather hinder him ; but that on the contrary
faith can bring on the way to obtain all this
fruit. Let the soul who doubts if he indeed
has faith, and may have it, consider that, while
his feeling of unworthiness and guilt causes so
much darkness and anxiety in the depths of his
spirit, it is only in this poverty of the soul that
faith can flourish, and that it is by this means
that he will be driven to his Lord. And let

the soul who believes never forget that this must be one of the indispensable fruits and proofs of the sincerity of his faith, namely, a constantly growing self - abhorrence and a becoming less in his own eyes, according to the word of the Lord to His people: "I will establish my covenant with you, that ye may be ashamed, when I shall make atonement for you, for all that thou hast done, saith the Lord" (Ezek. xvi. 61–63).[1]

Reader, why do you not believe? Surely it is not that you will still wait for more penitence and contrition of heart. Ah, no: this last grace, too, is always a fruit of faith. Believe to-day in the grace of Him who comes to you. All that is lacking in you must stir you up to this. With Him you receive everything that you are going to seek elsewhere in vain.

[1] Dutch Version

CHAPTER XIII

The Fear of Faith

" By faith, Noah moved with godly fear prepared an ark."—HEB. xi. 7.

THERE are many who suppose that, when the word of God says, "Blessed is the man that feareth always," it is commending a disposition that is at variance with the rest and assurance that are given by faith. And they thus regard this unbelief as a sort of virtue: they fear this great and holy God, and they fear their own weakness and unfaithfulness, and they dare not believe. This view is altogether out of harmony with the word of God; for the word teaches us that fear and confidence must go hand in hand with each other. "Many shall see it and fear, and shall trust in the Lord" (Ps. xl. 3), "Ye that fear the Lord, trust in the Lord" (Ps. cxv. 11), "Behold, the eye of the Lord is upon them that fear Him, upon them that hope in His mercy" (Ps. xxxiii. 18). Fear

and confidence go in union: the one increases
the other.

Very clearly is this truth set before us in the
history of Noah. "By faith Noah, being
warned of God concerning things not seen as
yet, moved with godly fear, prepared an ark.
The fear was partly the fruit of his faith, and
partly a motive to make his faith active in the
building of the ark. He believed the announce-
ment of the avenging flood, and feared; feared
in view of the destruction that was to overtake
his fellow-men, and in view of the holy God
from whom the judgment was to proceed. He
feared, and therefore he cleaved in strong faith
to the promise of the ark, and worked at it as
the only means of preservation. Fear and trust
were with him inseparable, the one indispensable
to the other.

Anxious soul, you fear the Lord, you fear
His holiness and His judgments, and you say
that it is out of veneration for Him that you do
not dare to believe. You say that you are too
unworthy in the presence of such a holy and
dreadful God to appropriate the right of being
called His child, and of speaking to Him with
confidence. O that you knew how grievously
you are mistaken. There is nothing that so
much tends to arouse in the Lord the sense of

dishonour and anger as unbelief—not believing
His word, that He has compassion on all the
unworthy. There is nothing on which God
so much sets His honour as His free grace and
His pity for the ungodly. You wound Him
in the most tender point when you doubt if
His grace is indeed for you, and so drag its
greatness and trustworthiness into doubt. O
souls, when you fear the Lord, pray, fear to
dishonour Him by unbelief.

But, no : you say that it is not the Lord, but
yourselves that you doubt. You fear on account
of your unfaithfulness, your insincerity. And
do you not then understand that it is just this
fear of yourselves that is the strongest argument
for your casting yourselves upon the Lord and
entrusting yourselves to Him. O soul, pray,
seek no longer something in yourselves ; for, if
you wait until you no longer fear for yourselves,
you will never come to Christ at all. God
never asks you for an engagement to be faithful
on which He can rely. No : He gives *you* a
promise of faithfulness on which you can rely.
And just because you fear your own unfaithfulness, you must place your confidence on
God's faithfulness. Herein just lies the glory
of free grace, that the sinner, who cannot trust
himself, who feels that in everything — in

faith, in humility, in earnestness, in sincerity —he comes far short, may yet surrender himself to the Lord as one who is utterly wretched, with confidence in the word that He certainly receives, and will keep such an one. Yea: it is he who fears on his own account that must trust in the Lord. This is the only remedy. He has nothing on which he can hope but the promise of God's compassion. Every thought of fear must be a new motive to confidence. So shall he learn to fear no more, according to the word of the psalmist: "Blessed is the man that feareth the Lord: his heart is established, he shall not be afraid" (Ps. cxii. 1, 8). He shall also learn to experience that the fear of the Lord then becomes through confidence the source, not of anxiety but of peace and growing power, according to that other word: "The Church, walking in the fear of the Lord and in the comfort of the Holy Ghost, was multiplied" (Acts ix. 31).

CHAPTER XIV

The Certainty of Faith

"**Looking** unto the promise of God, he wavered not through unbelief, being fully assured that what He had promised He was able also to perform."—ROM. iv. 20, 21.

ABRAHAM did not doubt. Glorious testimony to provoke us to jealousy, and thus to the imitation of his example. Therefore the word also gives us to know what the power was in virtue of which he obtained faith and brought all doubt to silence. The secret lay simply in the conviction: *What God has promised, He is able also to perform.* On this account he was assured, and whenever reflections and doubtings would arise, he always held before his eyes the incontrovertible argument: That which has been promised, God is able to perform. Hence it is that there stands written: "Without being weakened in faith, he considered his own body now as good as dead before Him whom he believed, even God, who quickeneth the dead and calleth the things that are not as

though they were" (Rom. iv. 19, 17, R.V.)
To every question, "How can these things be?"
there was his simple answer: "What God has
promised He is able also to perform. For the
Lord there is nothing too wonderful. It is not
my business to be anxious, and to say how God's
word can be fulfilled. The Lord will see to it."

My reader, you mourn over the power of your
doubts, and say that you cannot overcome them:
come, learn of Abraham how you can do this.
The first thing that is necessary is that you
understand and reflect what promise the Lord
has given you. If the Lord has given no
promises for you, then it cannot be your duty
to believe. But, as surely as the word says
"Believe," is there also a promise which you
must believe. To take only one out of the
thousands which are in the Scriptures, "The
Son of Man is come to seek and to save that
which was lost." God gives you the gracious
promise, and commands you to believe it with
all your heart. It is His will that you should
receive it as the truth that His Son has come for
all that are lost, hence also for you. He desires
that you should believe that His Son seeks you
and longs for you, and that His Son will save
you.

God wills that you should ponder this thought

and cherish it in your heart, until your whole
soul takes its stand or this truth : *Jesus seeks me,
lost as I am ; there is grace for me.* As soon as
you believe that, the Saviour begins to come
in to you.

If now you have reached this first point, if
you know that there is a promise also for you,
then the second duty is not to look into yourselves to know if there is hope that what you
expect will take place. As Abraham did not
regard his own body, which was already dead,
so must you not regard your own dead soul.
Although you feel yourself to be dead, powerless, insincere, very sinful, although you are
lacking in penitence, earnestness, and in all
else that you know you ought to have, still
act like Abraham : believe on God, who maketh
the dead alive, and calleth the things that are
not as though they were. Act like Abraham,
and cast down every doubt with the thought :
" What God has promised He is able also to
perform." Keep your mind occupied with this
certain truth : He is come to save that which
was lost, and there is no lost one so far lost that
Jesus cannot find him and cannot save him.

Once again, it comes simply to these two
points : know if there is a promise for you, lost
sinner ; if so, then cleave simply to this fact :

What has been promised He is able also to perform. "Lord, I believe; help thou mine unbelief. I will no longer dishonour Thee by doubtings: Thy power, Thy love, Thy faithfulness, I will adore and trust. I will venture to surrender my soul to Thee. Although I feel it not, I will believe it. Thou seekest and savest that which is lost. Lord, help: I do believe."

CHAPTER XV

The Glorifying of God by Faith

" He wavered not through unbelief ; but waxed strong through faith, giving glory to God. Wherefore also it was reckoned unto him for righteousness."—ROM. iv. 20, 22.

THE question is frequently asked by those who have not yet come to faith, and who on this account do not yet fully understand it, What, pray, may be the reason why faith is so highly esteemed by the Lord and is capable of such great things? The answer is simple : *It gives glory to God.* It humbles the sinner in the dust as one who deserves nothing and is capable of nothing, and must on this account present himself to God as dependent on the promises of a free compassion. It glorifies God in the acknowledgment of His power and love which will bestow redemption ; of His word and faithfulness also, since these are held to be so strong and glorious that the sinner, although he has nothing else, can commit himself to them. Faith sets God and man in the right relation to

one another—God on the throne of His sovereign
grace, from whom all must and shall come ; man
in his misery and nothingness, as one who has
nothing in himself but guilt and its curse.

In the other virtues of the Christian life,
such as humility and love, there is always something that is wrought in man, that he can feel,
and of which he might be able to boast.   True
faith on the other hand is the confession of utter
poverty and helplessness.   It says : " I have
nothing left, I can also do nothing.   I must now
simply remain silent to hear what God speaks,
to see what He will do, to receive what He will
give."   It is truly the attitude of a beggar, by
which man is laid in the dust.   And yet no
angel in heaven can give God so much honour as
faith, when out of the surrounding darkness and
sin and poverty it still relies on God and expects
from Him the certain fulfilment of that which
He has promised.

Alas ! how great is the foolishness of the
heart of man.   How many are there still, who
really imagine that they give glory to God by
their unbelief.   They fancy that, when they
mourn heavily over themselves and their misery,
telling how unworthy they are to appropriate
such grace because they have so deep a sense of
the greatness and holiness of God, this is to the

honour of God. On the contrary, it is really to
His dishonour: as if He were not sufficiently
gracious towards the unworthy, not sufficiently
powerful to rescue the utterly wretched, not
faithful to perform His word. No: faith alone
gives glory to God, for it sets no limits to the
Holy One of Israel. It has but one question,
What has God said? When it has once known
this, then it asks nothing further about possi-
bility or truth or anything else. The word of
God is enough for the soul. Like Abraham, it
gives glory to God by being strong in faith.

Beloved reader, it is a terrible sin to rob
God of His honour. By being unbelieving you
make yourself guilty of this offence. As God
has revealed Himself in the gospel more
gloriously than in the law, so is the sin of
unbelief in relation to the promises much more
dreadful than that of disobedience to the com-
mandments. For this reason, I entreat you,
believe what God says. Ask not what you are
or what you have, but if there is anything with
respect to which God will have it that you shall
now believe, or if there is any promise with
which He comes to meet the ungodly. Here is
one: "Christ died for the ungodly." Receive
that word, keep it in your heart, ponder and
believe it, and rest not until it abides as essential

truth with you, even as it is with God : "Christ is for the ungodly." Yes: this very day, O souls, give glory to the Lord, by going to Him as the gracious, almighty, and faithful Redeemer ; commit yourselves to His word, be strong in faith and thereby give glory to God, as you go to Him.

Anxious ones, in God's name, why do you not believe? This is the only thing that you are to do, the **only thing that God will** have —**only** believe.

CHAPTER XVI

The Power of Faith

"By faith even Sarah herself received power since she counted Him faithful who had promised."—HEB. xi. 11.

SEE here again one of the examples, so simple and intelligible of what faith is: "She counted Him faithful who had promised." There was a time when Sarah doubted, for she looked to nature, and it said to her that she should no longer bear. Through the repeated promises of the Lord she was nevertheless led to look to Him who had given the promises, and keeping in mind His divine faithfulness she found there was no alternative for her but to believe; and the only account which she could give of the supernatural expectation of faith was this: "He is faithful that promised" (Heb. x 23).

The same way must still be followed by those Christians who desire to be liberated from their doubts and to reach the blessed experiences of the life of faith. We must learn to have done with the reasonings of the understanding; with the questions which nature would have first answered, such as, "How can these things be?", "Whereby shall I know it?", with calculations as to whether our own wisdom and power are perchance sufficient to bring us where we must know; and we must hold ourselves content with the view expressed in this sentence: "He is faithful that promised." The only thing which one has to ask is this, "Is there a promise also for me?" If the word of God gives us the answer: "This is a faithful saying and worthy of all acceptation, that Jesus Christ came into the world to save sinners of whom I am the chief," then that is sufficient to bring us down before the Lord and to make us expect that He will perform the promise to us: "He is faithful that promised."

O, if souls would only keep themselves occupied with the consideration of God's faithfulness, how would unbelief be ashamed. Whenever anxious feelings multiply in you, and you fear for yourself and your work, go, O soul, bow down in silent meditation and adoration before your God as the faithful One, until your whole spirit become filled with the thoughts and the peace that spring from this attribute. Go over all the assurances in the Scriptures, so glorious and clear, that the unchangeable One

Himself shall fulfil His counsel, and that He simply desires of souls the stillness which observes and expects the performance. Take counsel with the believers of the old and new covenants, reflect on their ways and their leadings, and they will tell you with one accord that their strength and their peace have been— the faithfulness of God.   O, pray, accustom yourself, every day, with every promise of God that you read, with every prayer that you make for the attainment of what God has spoken to you of, with every fear that arises in you as to whether you shall be indeed partaker of the offered salvation,—pray, accustom yourself to fasten your eye undividedly on that word, to let your whole heart be filled with it: "He is faithful that promised." And, above all, even when you are not yet able to appropriate everything to yourselves, forget not to praise and to thank God for His faithfulness; praise and adore Him as the Faithful One: adoration will confirm you in faith in Him. Nor must you set your hope on the divine faithfulness only when you are taking the first steps on the way of conversion, seeking for forgiveness and acceptance, but, especially in the midst of the struggle, to be confirmed unto the end and to be unreprovable in the day of our Lord Jesus. It is

with his eye fixed on this hope that Paul says
"God is faithful, through whom ye were called
into the fellowship of His Son Jesus Christ"
(1 Cor. i. 8, 9); just as in that glorious work
about sanctification that finds so little belief,
"The God of peace sanctify you wholly," he
also immediately adds: "Faithful is He that
calleth you, who will also do it" (1 Thess. v.
23, 24).

It was by this faith, this loyal esteem of the
faithfulness of her God and reliance upon it,
that Sarah received power to bear. So far is
this faith also from leading to sluggishness and
indifference that it will increase activity. It
teaches the soul to wait upon God spiritually
and earnestly, that He may point out to it what
it must do, and that it may learn by experience
to understand the deep significance of that word:
"Work, for God worketh in you." Believing in
His faithfulness also to work in it, it has courage
to work after Him. "By faith she received
power, since she counted Him faithful who had
promised."

CHAPTER XVII

The Childship of Faith

"As many as received Him, to them gave He the right to become children of God, even to them that believe on His name."—JOHN i. 12.

*T*HE *receiving of the Lord Jesus* is here said to be the same as *believing on His name*. One receives Him as soon as one believes, yea through believing on His name. His name is always Jesus, Saviour. As soon as the soul believes this, and on this account looks on Him as the man who certainly saves the sinner, it not merely thinks: "He can do this, yet I know not if it will take place with me," but it regards Him as a Saviour given by God also for himself, and thus believes on His name that it essentially expresses what Jesus is,—as soon as, I say, the sinner does this, he receives Him. He acknowledges Him in His grace as Jesus, appropriates Him in the faith which says, "He is also for me"; he receives Him as a gift bestowed by God, set before Him to be appropriated, receives

Him as that which His name signifies—Saviour, the only and perfect Saviour. He acknowledges that in himself there is nothing good nor ever shall be; he foresees manifold unfaithfulness and backsliding; he feels himself to be wholly powerless: but he receives Jesus as a Saviour, as one who undertakes the whole work, who from day to day will continue that work and accomplish it in the leading, the keeping, and the sanctification of the soul. And according as he believes further in that name, in the absolute truth, the far-reaching signification, the inexhaustible power of that name, in this same measure does he receive Jesus more perfectly in the riches of His manifold blessings, and experience how true it is: *Jesus saves.* He gives power to men to become the children of God, enables them also to say, through the Spirit, "Abba, Father," and with all the dispositions of children — confidence, fear, love, obedience—to rejoice in God's fatherly love.

Reader, are you seeking salvation? O, then, receive Jesus. He is *offered* to you by God as a Saviour. *Receive Him as a gift* of the Divine love; acknowledge Him as really also for you; believe that, with His name, it is the full truth that the work of saving a sinner may well be entrusted to Him; receive Him in that faith,

coupled with the simple surrender of yourselves,
dead and wretched as you are, into His hands,
and be assured that you shall not come out
deceived. Away with all doubtings. In the
name of God I ask you, as upright dealing is
for you indispensable to being saved : Do you
believe in the name of Jesus, or do you not
believe in it? Do you believe in the name
JESUS, given by the true God to His Son, in
order that you may build your hope upon it?
O sinner, pray, believe that the name, Jesus, is
divine truth. Come, say to-day, "Yes: He is
the Saviour of that which was lost"; no longer
shut Him out, but receive Him in the heart,
with simple faith in His word, *I am Jesus.*
Begin with this, continue with this, go forward
with this, believe evermore in the name JESUS ;
receive Him with this, and He shall give you
power to become a child of God. Here once
more what God says to you to-day, "As many
as received Him "—thousands on earth and in
heaven can corroborate the statement that it is
really so—"to them gave He the right to become children of God, even to them that believe
on His name."

CHAPTER XVIII

The Surrender of Faith

"First they gave their own selves to the Lord."—2
COR. viii. 5.

IN the word of His promise, through the
gracious working of His Spirit, the Lord
gives Himself to us; through faith we receive
Him, and we know that He is ours.   This faith,
as the outgoing of the soul to Jesus to meet
Him, is at the same time a surrender to Him.
We can never receive the Saviour and His grace
without at the same time surrendering ourselves
to Him, to be sealed and filled with salvation.
And as faith knows that the Lord is ours, because His word tells us that He gives Himself
to us, so it also knows that He receives us as
His own, because His word assures us of that.

Faith has thus two sides: the believing reception of the Lord Jesus with all that He
gives, and the believing surrender of the soul
with all that it has to the Lord.   The one
cannot be without the other.   I take Jesus as

my King to rule over me, **as a** Saviour to free
me from sin; He cannot perform His work in
me, if I do not surrender myself to Him.   Confidence in Jesus is thus at the same time a
committal of one's self to Him.

Anxious soul, see here again the simplicity
of faith.   If you wish to know what you have
to do, the answer is, Give yourself to the Lord
Jesus.

Give yourself to the Lord Jesus, *just as you
are.*   You have to give yourself to Him, not as
an offering that is worthy of Him, as one who is
already His friend and on whom He can look
down with complacency.   No: you have to surrender yourself to Him as one that is dead,
whom He has to make alive, as an enemy whom
He must reconcile and forgive, as a sinner whom
He must save.   The multitude of your sins,
the corruption which you feel struggling within
you, the very insincerity of your coming to Him,
are thus no reason why you should not venture
to give yourself to Him.   No: just the reverse:
these are the proofs that you stand in need of a
Saviour; they are at the same time the tokens
given by the word of God of those in whose
behalf Jesus came   O sinner, just as you are,
surrender yourself to Jesus.

Surrender yourself also to Him *wholly and*

undividedly. Keep nothing back of what is
yours. Think not that He is to do one part of
the work and you the rest. No: submit entirely to His estimate of you. Although you
do not yet feel the power to make a separation
from all sins, although you still feel that the
heart is attached to one thing and another, and
will cleave to them, make confession of all this
before Him; for it is also through the confession
of sins that we surrender ourselves to Him.
Understand that the more you surrender yourself entirely to Him, the more completely is He
able to accomplish His work for you. Think of
His complete surrender for you and to you;
think of the claim of His love upon you and the
complete salvation with which He will fill you,
and let your surrender to Him be complete and
undivided.

And, above all, surrender yourself to Him *in
faith.* You have perchance given yourself to
Him ere this, but it brought you no peace, for
you did not know if the surrender was accepted
by Him. You would have a token from heaven,
a divine inspiration in your heart to tell you
that He had accepted you. And this was wrong.
He has said: "*Him that cometh unto Me, I will
in no wise cast out.*" God has said: "Return
ye, and I will receive you." When you sur-

render yourself to Jesus, you must believe that; in that word you must have sufficient. You are to take your stand upon it, because God speaks the truth. However wretched you are, however imperfect your surrender is, it must be a surrender of faith, of faith that He receives you, because He has said it. Although you find it difficult to believe that so firmly, although it seems to you very hazardous for so great a sinner, it is, nevertheless, your duty to believe that, when you surrender yourself to the Lord, He receives you. Do not set yourself above God. Do not say, I have done my part but I know not if God will do His. No: think of the word; say to the Lord that it is *on His promise* that you surrender yourself; day after day be occupied with the faithfulness of God's promise and you shall gradually come to the blessed certainty: He receives me. Yes: you shall even be able to say, He has received me.

CHAPTER XIX

The School of Faith

"O woman, great is thy faith; be it done **unto thee** even as thou wilt."—MATT. xv. 28.

A GREAT faith: all should know that there is nothing on earth so desirable. Many may wish to have it and may pray for it, and yet there are but few that come to it. And why? A principal reason is this: they will not walk in the way that leads to it; they are afraid of the school where that faith is taught. Or, they have very wrong ideas concerning the way to attain that great faith, as if, for instance, it were a gift which is bestowed at once. So perverse are their thoughts, that when the Lord is going to hear their prayers and is to lead them in another way than they had expected, they suppose that He is no longer caring for them. Come, all ye that long for more faith, learn from the Canaanite woman, how the Lord will bring you to it.

First of all, He will *try* you. The Canaanite

woman had a daughter possessed by a devil, and what a trial was not that to her? And so the Lord still sends His children trials of very different kinds. With one, it is trial in the physical life; with another, trial in the family; with another again it is inward vexation of soul; with still more it is hidden conflict with sin. But trial there must be; for so long as the flesh has everything agreeable and according to its inclination, the soul will never wholly and with power cleave to the Lord. It is by necessity that it is driven out to seek all its salvation in the Lord and to commit itself to Him. Blessed trial, the message of God to teach more faith, how many regard thee as the messenger of His wrath and aversion, instead of humbly suffering themselves to be led by thy hand to the Lord.

Further: when the Lord is to lead a soul to great faith, He leaves its *prayers unheard.* So it was with the Canaanite woman. He answered her not one word, and when He did at length reply to her, the answer was still more unfavourable than His silence. This is always the way. If the answer came immediately, how would the soul get acquainted with the Lord Himself. His gifts would occupy its attention so much that it would overlook the Lord Himself. It must first be put to the proof, whether it can take its stand

upon its Lord and what He has provided, without
any answer; whether He and His word are to
suffice for it; yea, whether it will, even when
His word appears to be opposed to it, still not
doubt His love, but rather commit itself to it.
A faith so great that it still cleaves to the Lord
in spite of apparent rejection: this precious
lesson, which is above all else acceptable to the
Lord, is learned and practised only in the conflict
of unheard but persevering prayer.

Once more: the soul that is to come to great
faith *must be humbled*. What a hard word for
the poor heathen woman: "It is not meet to
take the children's bread and cast it to the dogs."
But she suffers it to be well-pleasing to her, and
uses it as her strongest argument. She over-
comes the Lord with His own weapons and turns
His rejection into her plea: "Even the dogs eat
of the crumbs that fall under their master's
table." Do you also likewise: whenever, in
following the Lord, your sins are laid bare to you,
and your unworthiness held up before you, and
the word makes you feel that you are an ungodly
and accursed sinner, always answer with the
woman, "Yea, Lord, I am very wretched; all
that my heart testifies of sin is true: 'yet, yet
even the dogs eat'; and with such a Lord as
Thou art, there is overflowing grace even for the

most wretched." The deeper the root, the stronger the tree; the deeper the descent of humility, the stronger the faith; for then it leans, not half on itself, but wholly on the Lord.

See here, thou, my soul, Jesus' school for faith. Let it not grieve you, if the lessons are sometimes heavy; He has told you of this beforehand. But hold fast this conviction: when my soul is brought into trial, when my sin and unworthiness become more distinct, and press me the deeper down, I shall look upon all this as the way along which the all-loving Jesus is to lead me to that life of faith, in which He takes such delight; and when I am dispirited, I shall read again the story of the Canaanite, and I shall be strengthened by the glorious victory and reward of her conflict of faith. The more difficult the school, the more glorious the prize; "Be it done unto thee, even as thou wilt."

CHAPTER XX

The Word of Faith

"So belief cometh of hearing, and hearing by the word of Christ."—ROM. x. 17.

HERE is the simple answer to the question, How does faith arise in the soul? The Spirit, the author of faith, uses for this purpose a means, and that means is the word. It cannot be otherwise. The Spirit does not work apart from the faculties of man, but by means of them. His supernatural power makes use of the natural gifts which remain to man after his sin, renews and sanctifies them. By awakening desire, He bends the will; by presenting the loveliness of Jesus, He works upon the affections; and thus also, when He works faith, He does so by presenting the truth, in order thereby to awaken confidence.

I take it for granted that my reader is one who has been awakened; who, desiring to be saved, is looking out for rescue; who longs to be freed from his sin, and asks, How, pray, do

I come to faith in Jesus? The answer is, By
the word. But what am I to do with the word?
Do with it what you should do with any ordinary
message which you cannot at once believe. Suppose that tidings is brought to you of a great
inheritance which comes to you. You had not
been expecting it, and cannot believe that so
great happiness and wealth have fallen to your
lot. What are you to do? You will inquire
if the messenger is trustworthy. If you are
sure of this point, in order to obtain all certainty, you will ask him once and again and
again to say that you are the person intended;
or if he has brought a letter of conveyance
or a will, you will read it repeatedly.
And thus, by explanation and confirmation
of his message, you will become convinced
and will believe. This is just: faith is by the
word.

Not otherwise is it in divine things.

When the message comes to you, *Jesus is a
Saviour for sinners, also for you*, do you ask if
you are to believe Him who speaks? The
answer is, Yes: for He is the true God. Do
you ask if there is no misunderstanding, or if
you are really the person intended? Yes: for
the message is to every sinner. Then does it
become your duty to listen earnestly to the

message; to ask repeatedly, yea unceasingly—
for the matter is of moment—Shall I or shall
I not believe? And the more you simply take
the word, read and read again the message of
God, contemplate one after another the promises
with which God has made it sure that the
Saviour is for every sinner, the sooner shall
you feel constrained to say, It is true; God says
it; I must believe it.

O, poor sinner, pray cease to ask what your
own heart feels, as one who would be saved.
Cease to seek the ground of faith in yourselves.
Attend now to the word: Jesus is the Saviour
of sinners. Listen to it again and yet again.
Let your soul become occupied the whole day
with the thought: God says it; it must be. And
continue with this, the more wretched and dark
the condition of your heart may be. Ask simply
from day to day, What says the word? Take
and carry that word in your heart, and you shall
speedily experience that "faith is by the word."
And so far from making you think that faith is
thus a work of your own power will such activity
be, that you shall acknowledge that it is by the
word the Spirit works. Your use of the word
gives you reason, gives you right, to hope for
His help. You shall experience how little
faith is merely a reasoning of the intellect,

but at the same time how faithful God is to
bestow His grace on the use of means, and to
crown with His blessing the soul that honours
His word.

CHAPTER XXI

The Thanksgiving of Faith

"So walk in Him, established in your faith, abounding in thanksgiving."—COL. ii. 17.

THE idea which is here expressed by the apostle is, that where faith is active and growing it will always go coupled with thanksgiving; as it stands written: "Then believed they His words; they sang His praise." As faith stirs up to thanksgiving, so it exercises a reactive influence; it in turn strengthens faith. Faith and thanksgiving belong to one another and keep one another. The more I believe, the more I shall thank; the more I thank, the more I shall believe. The lack of faith is the reason that men give thanks so little; the neglect of thanksgiving hinders and weakens faith. This is a fault to which too little attention has been paid and from which many a one suffers great loss. Let us consider it for a moment.

The reason why thanksgiving has the effect of

increasing faith is manifest. Faith has its
greatest power in the fact that in believing the
soul wholly forgets itself, and with undivided
energy looks to God and hears Him—goes out
wholly to Him. This is in like manner pre-
cisely the nature of thanksgiving, that in it the
soul must be entirely occupied with God, with
the contemplation of His goodness, the adoration
of His Godhead, the consideration of His ways,
the expression of His wonders. Accordingly,
the more the mind is exercised in this work, and
is taken up with the thought of all this, the
more shall there be fixed and rooted in it the
conviction that the Lord is truly a God on whom
it is its duty to rely. If thanksgiving, the
express mention of His omnipotence, His love,
His faithfulness, His perfection shall fill the
soul, the result cannot but be that the soul shall
suffer it to be concentrated on God. He that
has but a single word of such a God to build
upon has enough. In such thanksgiving the
soul will have its desires roused, its courage
strengthened, its inward devotion to Him
deepened. The shamefulness of its unbelief
will be very manifest as an offence against such
a God. The remembrance of unbelief, of my
unworthiness, my lack of love, my insincerity,
my weakness and my uncertainty as to whether

I shall remain faithful,—all this shall be utterly blotted out by what the thankful soul has expressed, namely, that God in His compassionate and omnipotent love is greater than all the force of sin and Satan. It cannot be otherwise, if thanksgiving increases faith. Hence that word: " Abounding in faith with thanksgiving."

And now I wish to ask you who here say that you are seeking the increase of faith this question, Are you really doing this by thanking God? If you are still unconverted, go and thank Him that you are still not in hell. O, what a wonder it is that in His longsuffering He has still borne with you and spared you. Thank Him for this. Thank Him that He gave His Son Jesus for sinners. Yes: although you are not yet able to say that He is yours, fall upon your knees and thank God for His unspeakable gift to this sinful world and also to you. Thank Him for His gracious promise which has also come to you. O sinner, though you have as yet received little or nothing for yourself, pray be not silent, but adore and speak of His wonderful compassion. Let this be a daily work with you. Keep yourself intensely occupied with it: let your soul abide in contemplating what God is, what He has done, what He has promised He will do; how gracious,

how faithful He is and **how** mighty to deliver **and** endeavour, however imperfectly, to express this on your knees before Him. In every acknowledgment of your bitter misery, thank Him that He is God ; confess before Him that He is great and good. This thanksgiving will teach your soul that you may calmly confide in God. And, throughout the whole conflict of faith, you will often have to say that, when everything looked utterly dark and your wretchedness was very deep, if you but rendered thanks for what God was, hope then once more revived in your soul. Whatever else fails you, this always remains— a God to praise. Never was your case so wretched, that you had nothing more left to be thankful for. Only put this remedy to the proof: in the midst of all that is dark, grievous, and incomprehensible for the soul, only begin to praise, and your praising shall speedily merge in believing. Praising and believing are one.[1]

[1] The Dutch here admits of a play upon words : ' Loven en gelooven zijn één."

CHAPTER XXII

The Offence of Faith

"And Elisha sent a messenger unto him, saying, Go and wash in Jordan seven times."—2 KINGS v. 10.

THE story of Naaman's healing has at all times served as a striking illustration of the way of faith, with all the humbling, yea offensive, features that it has for the natural heart, of which Naaman himself is to us so clear an example.

The answer of Naaman when he received the message of the prophet—how entirely is it in accordance with the expectation of nature, which is so fain to see something, so fain to receive something in the shape of external ceremonies: "Behold, I thought, He will surely come out to me, and stand, and call on the name of the Lord his God, and wave his hand over the place, and recover the leper." How completely emerges here the inclination of the seeker for healing, who would have a sensible, visible, impressive revelation of the Lord's power; and who, when a servant is sent with *the simple message of faith,* turns away disappointed, as if this were no answer to his prayer.

And then the contents of the message—to wash in Jordan. If water could do it, were not the rivers of Damascus larger than the Jordan, were not their waters better than all the waters of Israel? He did not know that it was not the water, but the power of God through His word with the water. And in like manner the seeker for salvation cannot under-stand that it must just be faith by which he is to be cleansed. Are there not the waters of a deep and inward penitence, the streams of sincere humility, the loyalty of an inner love? Why is it, pray, that faith is to be named above these? How many there are that go and set their dis-position before and above mere simple faith; as if God called not that which is weak and de-spised, and indeed nothing; as if He had not chosen faith as the way in which man, as capable of no achievement, was to receive every-thing out of free compassion.

But, more than all else, the washing seven times was sure to prove a stumbling-block, unless he had previously been taught to submit to the obedience of faith. If the waters were good, why was not one washing sufficient? If

the healing did not take place at the fifth or
sixth time, why should it occur just at the
seventh time? Reason was thoroughly entitled
to inquire in this fashion. But faith cannot
insist on an answer to these questions, and
at the same time obeys "according to the word
of the man of God." This submission should
become to us a very significant instance of the
longsuffering of faith. It should remind us
how faith is to hold out, although it sees not
the least token of alteration or healing. It
should teach us the lesson which is learned with
so much difficulty that there must be a continual repetition of the act of faith, cleaving
fast to the word of God, until He bestows the
blessing.

O soul, seeking for salvation, learn here your
way. It is with submission to that which does
not appear to you the best means, which seems
to you too small and trifling for such a great
result, it is by the continuous repetition of what
at the outset seems fruitless, that you are called
on to persevere in faith. Pray, understand it,
faith is God's way. It was He that devised it,
and not man. On this account it is a stumbling-
block to every Naaman, until he learns, as one
that is helpless, to bow beneath the word of
God. Submit yourself to God and receive what

He says, that "he that believeth shall be saved." Go every day *to the word* and its streams of living water. Although it seems to you somewhat trifling to wash there, to plunge and bathe in it, to receive from it this or that promise, and to do the very same thing every day anew, without experiencing any healing, yet hold on. Persevere, and the blessed result shall be like that of Naaman. "His flesh came again like unto the flesh of a little child," he was as one born a second time, "and he was clean." You also shall be born again by the living word, and be cleansed from your sin. It does not lie in you, nor even in the word regarded in itself, but in the faithfulness of God, who has said: "**He that believeth shall not be ashamed.**"

CHAPTER XXIII

The Stability of Faith

" Now faith is the assurance of things hoped for."—
HEB. xi. 1."[1]

MANY people think that faith is something
which at its best is but very uncertain :
not so certain, for example, as sight or hearing.
They appear to think that faith is a sort of
imagination by which we must take pains to be
assured in our own hearts that we shall be saved.
The result of this erroneous conception is that
they often attempt to exercise it, but find no
rest in it, or perhaps even come to regard all
assurance of faith as conjecture, self-deception,
or presumption. They do not understand what
faith is.

The Epistle to the Hebrews might have taught
them. There faith is represented as the highest
certainty, as a sure foundation on which one
can build and safely trust oneself. In faith there

[1] The Dutch version has, "Now faith is a firm foundation of the things which we hope for," etc.

is nothing that moves or can be moved: faith
is a strong basis, and that indeed for the simple
reason that faith depends upon what stands
more firmly than rocks or mountains, namely,
the word of God. Heaven and earth shall pass
away, but the word of God endures to eternity.
And on this account it is that to come to rest,
peace, and stability, the soul has simply to ask,
"What has God said?" Is there anything that
God has commanded me to believe? Has He
spoken anything that is directed to every sinner,
and that every sinner is bound to believe? If
so, then it is my duty to search out this and to
receive it as being the word of the true God,
and therefore sure and certain.

And what is it, then, that every sinner is to
believe? Simply this—that Christ has been
given by God also to him as a Saviour. "This
is a faithful saying and worthy of all acceptation,
that Jesus Christ is come into the world to save
sinners:" all sinners without distinction, even
the chief. Let the sinner that longs to be saved
only hold fast that truth, and be occupied with
it. Let him go out of himself, so as to be
hemmed in with this thought, until his heart
be filled with it: Jesus is come to save sinners,
even me; Jesus is given by God also to save
me: Christ is certainly for me. Not because I

have believed all this or have been converted; no, but because I am an ungodly one. And, whether I believe it or not, it remains truth that Christ is offered by God also to me. Before I believe it, it is the truth: the truth of it thus does not depend on anything in me that is yet to take place. The truth of it is grounded on the fact that God has said it. I have, therefore, nothing to do but to hear according to the word of God, and to receive it in my soul, until it becomes with me a settled conviction: it must be true, Christ is a Saviour also for me, for God has said it. Every questioning in the form of, Are you already converted? or, Are you worthy of it? or, Are you indeed sincere? I bring to silence with the simple answer: Whoever or whatever I may be, Christ is for the sinner, is also for me. And according as I day by day accustom myself simply to ask, Am I sure that *God* has said it? shall I experience that faith is a firm foundation. Standing on this basis, I cannot waver, but I come to an ever clearer insight into the truth that faith is nothing but a receiving and committing of oneself to the word of the true God. Hence it cannot be otherwise than that "faith is a firm foundation."

And now, anxious one, why do you not

believe? O, faith is no imagination that you too are a chosen one, but a laying of yourself down on the immovable rock of the word of the Lord. "God loved the world," "Christ died for the ungodly"; and now He comes to ask you— see to it, I entreat you, that you give Him an answer: "If I speak the truth to you, why do you not believe?"

CHAPTER XXIV

The Justification of Faith

" We reckon therefore that a man is justified by faith apart from the works of the law."—ROM. iii. 28.

THE Lord has revealed to us two ways, which should be able to lead us to Him and salvation. Along the one the *law* leads us, along the other *grace*. Both ways are good and come from God: yet there is after all only one of the two for us to use, by reason of our weakness. The law is good for those who have the power to obey and to follow it. Grace is the way for those who are powerless and can accomplish nothing. The law demands and must be fulfilled: grace gives and needs simply to be received. The law says, "Do this and thou shalt live"; grace says, "Believe and thou shalt be saved." The law demands works, yet gives no strength to produce them: grace asks for faith, which it also of its own power awakens by its promises—faith, which is nothing but the acknowledgment of weakness and a consent to be willing to receive everything for nothing. The law directs me to the height, to a mountain too steep to climb: grace to the valley, where I have only to sink down to be preserved.

Of the utmost importance is it that I should know well the distinction betwixt these two ways, choose the right one, and walk in it. For in our present sinful condition there is only one of these ways that is still really of service to us, although man on the contrary would just very fain walk in the other. Well is it for us that God has left us in no doubt as to which one is wished for and approved of by Him.

It was especially the Apostle Paul whom God chose to point out to us clearly the way of salvation—as he has done most fully in his Epistle to the Romans. The conclusion of his argumentation we have in the text quoted at the head of this chapter. He had shown how all mankind, Jews as well as heathen, had missed the glory of God. They could not fulfil, they did not wish to fulfil, the law of God. The law must be perfectly obeyed, otherwise it works only wrath. The law knows nothing of *grace*, only of right. God has searched the world, and

there was none righteous, not even one. By
the law every mouth was stopped, and the whole
world made guilty before God. It was a
declaration of the law itself, "By the works of
the law shall no flesh be justified" (Rom. iii. 20).
"But the righteous shall live by faith." That
the Lord Jesus had proclaimed. By His death
God had reconciled the world. He had allowed
the punishment and the demands of the law to
be fulfilled. He has permitted an everlasting
and infinite righteousness to be brought in.
For nothing had God suffered it to be offered :
without price and without money is this
righteousness ours, through the free gift of God.
In the case of the corrupt, curse-deserving, and
powerless sinner, there can be no talk of service
or works: only of faith, "Submission to the
righteousness of God." Where that faith in
Jesus and the word of His grace is found, there
is the sinner made partaker of the righteousness
of God, faith being simply the eye to see it as
it was offered, the hand to receive it, and the
activity for appropriating it for himself. He
that believeth is justified.

What folly, then, is it still to look to one's
own works or merit. Sinner, are you resolved
to work? Then must you keep the whole law,
and that perfectly ; and thus you shall certainly

be condemned.   Do you desire to be justified?
Only believe in Christ and His righteousness, in
God and the promises of His grace, as intended
also for you.   By that faith man **is** justified
without the works of the law.

CHAPTER XXV

The Works of Faith

" **Ye see** that by works a man is justified, **and not**
only by faith."—JAS. ii. 24.

IT has often been supposed that there was
opposition betwixt this utterance of James
and the doctrine of Paul. It is to be nevertheless acknowledged at once that this is not the
case, when one reflects that the works of which
Paul speaks are entirely different from those
which James intends. Paul always speaks of
the works of the law: James has his eye upon *the
works of faith. The works of the law* are those
which are done out of the personal power of man,
in the direction of fulfilling the law of God in
order to merit the favour of God and make himself worthy of it. Of these the word of God says,
that man is justified without the works of the
law. He can do nothing that is good or meritori-
ous: all that comes from him is impure and
deserving of wrath. On the contrary, *the works
of faith* of which James speaks are those **which**

must be done for the confirmation and the perfecting of faith, and thus out of the power which God gives and not to merit anything. They serve to manifest that which faith has received from free grace. They follow upon conversion, while the works of the law can only precede this change. The works of the law will be able to glorify man: the works of faith give God all the honour; for they are done in the acknowledgment of personal unworthiness. Works and faith go together, as being both fruits of grace and tokens of the renewing of the mind; faith as the root of the works, the works as the perfecting of faith.

In this way it can now be clearly understood what the word of God means, when in one passage it says: "To him that worketh not but believeth, his faith is reckoned for righteousness," and then again insists on works. The works which are done apart from faith, as an endeavour to make ourselves worthy of God's favour and thus keep us back from faith, the reception of God's free grace, are not to be done: they are abominable in the eyes of God: "He that worketh not is justified." The works which are done with and in faith, while the soul in the sense of its unworthiness commits itself to the gracious promises of God, just because it hopes

or knows that the Lord receives it apart from
its merits, and seeks to praise Him for them,
are acceptable to God, and must be done, the
more the better.   And it is of these that it is
said that "man is justified by works": they are
the manifestation of faith and actual fruit-bearing,
and not merely of a faith that continues inactive,
and is thus dead.

Let the soul which seeks to come to Jesus in
faith thus understand what it is to think of
works.   As soon as it begins to look upon its
works as the ground of merit, as soon as it
begins to say in fear, "My works are too small,
too trifling, too sinful for me to be received," it
must at once remember that "man is justified
without works."   No sin or ungodliness of
which you have been guilty ought to keep you
back from the hope of grace.   Yet, on the other
side, in order that the soul may not perhaps sit
down in idle inactivity, in order that it may not
go on in sin while it relies upon grace, let it be
remembered that as soon as the first beginnings
of the desire for grace awake within us—this,
if it is sincere, will necessarily show itself active
in the doing of God's will.   We shall be able
to pray with confidence and in truth, "forgive
us our debts," only when at the same time we
just as heartily endeavour to say, "as we forgive

our debtors"; just as John writes, "Let us not love in word, neither with the tongue but in deed and truth. Hereby shall we know that we are of the truth, and shall assure our heart before Him"; and, "If our heart condemn us not, we have boldness toward God." (Compare further 1 John iv. 22, as also Psalm xviii. 22–27.) Thus we learn to understand rightly the word, "work for God worketh in you," that is, by faith; and our works become the lovely evidences of His heavenly grace, the foretokens of His everlasting favour.

CHAPTER XXVI

The Obedience of Faith

"**By** faith Abraham, when he was called, obeyed to go out."—HEB. xi. 8.

BELOVED soul, you still say that you would fain believe, that it is your earnest and sincere desire to belong to the people of the Lord. You are nevertheless kept back, for what reason you yourself do not really know. Perhaps it is because it is not yet quite clear to you what you have to do when you believe. You do not yet understand the simplicity of faith, nor see that it is something which you can and must do without any even the least delay. Let us try to understand this by the example of the father of the faithful.

The Lord had said to Abraham: "Go thou out of thine own land to the country which I shall show thee." In this calling of Abraham, we find a divine command and a divine promise. The command is, "*Go thou out of thine land*": the promise is, "*to a country which I shall show thee."* By faith, says Paul to the Hebrews, he obeyed. Had he not believed the promises, had he not believed that the Lord would certainly bring him to that unknown land, he would surely never have gone out. His faith in the promise was his power for obedience to the command. He did not first go out of his land to become a believer thereby; for had he not first believed that he should find that foreign country he would never have had the courage to leave his fatherland. He first believed, and afterwards he went out.

God calls you also, my reader, to go out of the life of sin and to leave the world behind; but it is as if the call did not succeed with you. You are afraid that you shall never reach heaven. It is as if you had not the courage and the strength to tread that way. It is indeed no wonder. Abraham too would never have had the courage to abandon everything, and to undertake that long journey, had he not held fast the word of God: "The country which I shall show thee." Every consideration of the sacrifice, the folly, the dangers of going to an unknown land is overcome by the thought: "I go to a country which God will show me." Faith was his strength. Faith must also be your strength. Like Abraham, you too must learn to cleave to the word: "The Lord will bring you thither."

"But I have not received the promises," you cry. My reply is, You have indeed received the promises. God is not so unrighteous as to say to anyone that he must go to heaven without the promise that He will bring him thither. He has given you Jesus to show you the country, and to lead you on the way thither. He does not say, "Repent ye," without pointing to Jesus whom He ordained to give repentance. He does not say, "Abandon sin, and be saved," without at the same time saying, "Jesus frees and saves from sin." And it is only in the strength of this faith that you shall enter heaven. Therefore, soul, observe the calling of God: pray, understand that Jesus will do all for you: receive Him this day as the guide on the way given by God. However wretched you are, just simply believe that it is truth that God has given His Son Jesus also to you to save you. Be willing and acknowledge Him as your Saviour. Rejoice in the thought: God has given Him to the sinner and thus also to me. And although you still feel nothing in yourself, grasp firmly this thought the whole day: carry it round with you in the midst of all your work and over it: *It is certainly true, God has given*

Jesus also to me, to save me. This simple thought is faith. Hold fast by it, thank God for it: it will speedily send forth roots in you, and you shall rejoice in the assurance: Jesus is leading me to heaven. By this faith, you also, having been called, shall be obedient.

CHAPTER XXVII

The Nutriment of Faith

"A day's portion every day."—Ex. xvi. 4.

"I WILL rain bread from heaven for you; and the people shall go out and gather a day's portion every day, that I may prove them whether they will walk in my law or no." In these words we have announced to us what the rule is for the maintenance of the spiritual life, the law for the growth and increase of the life of faith. This law is in no respect different from that which we observe in the natural life every day. Every man knows how the little child is fed so as to grow up a strong man, how the strong man is supplied with nourishment so as to maintain his strength. The daily regular use of a little food gives man strength of body. Thus also is it with everything in nature: the little tree becomes large, the poor man becomes rich, the grandest building rises from its foundation, the longest journey can be performed, not

with great and violent strides, but by the silent, persevering faithfulness, which does not despise **the** little, invisible progress of every day, but uses it to reach the appointed goal.

"A day's portion every day," the general rule of the natural life prevails also in the spiritual; and yet there are so many Christians who, by not acknowledging this, suffer dreadful loss. They imagine that great exertion of strength **at** particular times, that fervent prayers when **we** feel ourselves stirred up, are the means of securing the increase and the flourishing of the soul's life. But the golden rule, "a day's portion every day," the day by day, regular continuance in the use of food, whereby the soul obtains **its** growth, they do not understand. They have not yet apprehended the lesson that faith and the life of faith must have nourishment, daily bread; and that with the promise, "I will rain bread from heaven," there stands the command: "The people shall gather **a** day's portion every day that I may" (this clause is added just for this very end) "prove them whether they will walk in my law or no."

Beloved reader, have **you** not often mourned over the unstable and changeable character **of** your spiritual life; have you **not** often wondered how it comes about that your **days of**

hope are so shortlived, and asked on all sides
what you had first to do that it might be otherwise with you, that your faith might abide
and increase? Would it surprise you that you
should be weak, if your body remained without
food for a couple of days, and that every time
afresh? And is it then to surprise you that
your faith should not be living, firm, and strong,
if you do not faithfully partake of *the word of
God?* That is the nutriment of faith: from it
and from it alone does faith draw its strength.
"Man shall live by every word that cometh
from the mouth of God." Confess that you
too often yield to this and that worldly circumstance, to idleness and apathy, and neglect
the hidden use of God's word, or use it so
hastily and superficially that your soul is not
nourished. No wonder that you have to mourn
over a leanness in your soul. Begin to-day
and henceforth let no day pass by without
eating of the heavenly manna, the word of
God and the living Christ in the word.
Receive the word in faith. God gave manna
every day in the waste wilderness up till the
home-coming in Canaan: if we go out and
gather, there will be in the word, for every new
day, instruction, strengthening, purification, and
salvation. And he who with faithful per-

severance continues day by day in the use of
the word, even when he does not at once observe
the blessing that flows from it, shall experience
that the increase of faith, although it be un-
observed and slow, is yet certain and sure.

CHAPTER XXVIII.

The Tenderness of Faith

" And they gathered it morning by morning, every man according to his eating : and when the sun waxed us hot, it melted."—Ex. xvi. 21.

IN the silence and coolness and secrecy of the night God gave the manna : in the freshness and quickening of the morning hour the people had to go out to gather it. It was thus the first work of every day to receive bread from God's hand ; for, when the sun waxed hot, it melted, and was no longer to be found. Not in the glow of the midday sun, nor in the press and bustle of the day, did they receive this hidden manna, but in the charming coolness of the morning, ere the mind was ensnared by the seductions of the world.

Lovely and instructive image of the way in which God still ministers to faith its nutriment. And I remain convinced that there are many that seem to be sincerely longing for confirma-

tion of faith, while they have not become partakers of it, because they do not go in search
of it betimes. How many are there, pray, by
whom the reading of the Bible is continued
only in the evening? After the freshness of
the morning hour and the strength of the day
have been devoted to the world, they come in
the evening, in weariness of mind and body,
to serve the Lord with the remnant of their
energies. No wonder that there is no blessing
enjoyed: the heart is weary, the tenderness of
the spirit and its receptiveness for the word is
dulled. On the other hand, are there not
many who are often content in the morning
with the general reading of the word in the
household, apart from private searching of the
Scriptures, or reflection or meditation with
prayer? This still yields little blessing. The
reading of a chapter once a day is, as a rule,
not sufficient. No: let all that truly desire to
increase in faith, see to it that they endeavour
in the morning hour to gather for the day
manna on which they can ruminate throughout
its course. He that goes out in the morning
without partaking of a portion of this nutriment comes home weary in the evening, with
but little desire to eat. And he who does not
in the morning first lay up the word in his

heart is not to be surprised if the world assumes the first and chief place in his heart, for he has neglected the only means of being in advance of the world. No: as the Lord gives us the night in order to throw off again the weariness of the day, and in the morning hour to make a new beginning with fresh spirit and energy, so must the believer take and devote to the Lord his first fresh and undiminished forces, and gather his manna while the blessing of the night's rest is upon him, and before the corruption of the world has again banished its lovely dew; for when the sun waxes hot, it melts. When the heat of the day has come, and temptation has first passed over the soul, all the gladness and trustfulness of the morning hour have also passed away. The life of grace will not endure the heat of the sun unless it be first strengthened by food.

"Cause me to hear thy lovingkindness in the morning." "O Lord, in the morning shalt Thou hear my voice; in the morning will I order my prayer unto Thee, and keep watch" (Ps. cxliii. 8; v. 3.) Such words point out to us what will be the attitude of the soul in him who is in earnest first and chiefly and with the whole heart to serve the Lord. With every morning hour he will taste the delightful experience of the word:

" His going forth is prepared as the daybreak (Hosea vi. 3.)

Reader, why do you not believe? Pray be faithful towards yourself and towards God. There is no piety in mourning over unbelief, unless you also lay aside everything that stands in the way of faith. If the irregular, superficial use of the word, if the giving of the first, the fresh, the best hours of the day and energies of the soul to the world and its service is the cause, then come, make a change in these points: morning by morning go and seek your God : He will not keep Himself hidden from you.

CHAPTER XXIX

The Hand of Faith

" Jesus said to the man that had his hand withered
. . . Stretch forth thy hand. And he did so : and his
hand was restored."—LUKE vi. 10.

ONE of the most common mistakes by which
souls are kept back from faith is that they
do not feel the strength for faith. They desire
first to feel faith living in themselves, and then
they would believe. But that the command to
believe should come to them while they do not
yet feel themselves prepared for it or in a position
to believe—this they do not comprehend. They
do not understand, because they have not
observed, what we experience or may see every
day, that readiness and ability for any work is
not given before the work but only through the
work, and thus after we begin to work. The
child that learns to run begins before he can
really do it, and learns in the midst of the effort.
The man that wishes to learn swimming goes
into the water while he cannot yet swim,

because he knows that, when he begins, he will in time learn to do it. And this law of nature has a still more glorious application in grace. God gives us commands for which we have previously no power, and yet requires obedience to them with full right; because He has said to us that when we submit, and set ourselves towards obedience, strength will be given along with this incipient activity. And this is the spirit in which we are to believe. Under the conviction of its unbelief, the soul must set itself to believe. In the assurance that power will be bestowed, it is yet to make a beginning: "Lord, I believe." In this action it is also to persevere and go forward.

Very strikingly are both aspects of this truth pictured to us in the case of the man with the withered hand. He feels his hand powerless, and yet Jesus says to him: "Stretch forth thy hand." He sees in the Saviour enough to convince him that He will not mock him, that He who gives this command will certainly never issue it without, at the same time, giving power to carry it out. He obeys and his hand is healed. O soul, the Lord Jesus who calls to you, "Believe in Me, as your Saviour," knows your helplessness. But it is just on this account that He speaks to you to rescue you from it.

With a voice of power He commands you,
"Believe in Me, that I am given by God to be
your Saviour: stretch out your hand to lay
hold of Me and to appropriate Me for yourself."
Listen to Him, be willing to obey Him;
remember that with the command He also gives
the strength; begin, although you do not yet
feel the power, and, although you can still do
nothing, say, like Martha: "I believe that Thou
art the Christ, the Son of God." Show that it
is your desire to believe, and that you are in dead
earnest about it; set your soul to attend to the
fact that He really speaks to you, and to hear
how charmingly attractive and kindly encour-
aging His voice is: "O thou unbelieving one,
believe in Me." As the man with the withered
hand obtained power to stretch it out at the
command of Jesus, so shall it be with you. The
command, "Believe," will no longer oppress you
with the thought, "I cannot do it," but encourage you to entertain the confidence: "Jesus
commands it, thus it is to be, thus it may be."
And if, with every inclination again to be discouraged, you look to Jesus and hear how
cheeringly He calls to you, "You may, you
must, you can believe in Me," your soul will be
strengthened with an ever-growing steadfastness
to entrust yourself to Him. In the endeavour

to believe, strength for it is given and exercised: the hand of faith will soon be entirely healed.

Soul, Jesus asks you, "If I speak the truth to you, why do you not believe?" He tells you the divine truth that He has come for you. He tells you the truth that your faith may be awakened thereby. I beseech you, understand this. See Him who here speaks: it is Jesus, the faithful and almighty Lover: hear His voice and be no longer unbelieving.

CHAPTER XXX

The Hindering of Faith

"Then cometh the devil and taketh away the word from their heart, that they may not believe and be saved."—LUKE viii. 12.

BY this word the Lord teaches us that whenever the devil is bent on keeping back anyone from salvation, he has merely to see to it that he keeps him back also from faith: he cannot then be prepared for salvation. And, on the other hand, in order to keep anyone back from faith, he has simply to take away the word from the heart: he does not then believe. And how dreadful is the thought that there are so many who, although they say that they desire to believe, yet work into the hand of the devil, so far as the word is concerned. To the devil it is a matter of small interest in what particular way this takes place, so long as he can take away the word out of the heart. In how many ways is this done.

In one case, by all manner of sin and unrighteousness. The love of sin cannot dwell together with the word. The heart cannot at the same time move towards God and away from God, cannot equally desire the word and sin. One or other of these must be cast out. Alas! how many thousand times does a sinner who said that he was seeking Jesus, and was desirous of believing, let slip the word which he has laid up in his heart in the morning, because he was not willing to say farewell to his sin, his anger, or lying, or deception, or envy, or impurity.

In another, the word is stifled by worldly cares and inclinations. It may be either the heavy sorrow and disquietude of one who has a difficult lot in the world, or it may be the temptation and preoccupation with the world that often springs from prosperity. How constantly it happens that the word is stifled, and thus taken away by love to the world.

Again, there are others from whom the devil takes away the word, through the soul's being occupied with itself and its sins. Instead of the heart being kept bent on the word of promise, the eye is fixed on its own inmost parts: the soul is so much taken up with its own feeling, its own wretchedness and weakness, with the effort to be converted in its own strength, that the word is loosely held, and so easily carried away.

And when one remembers how superficially the word is read, what little pains is taken to understand the word, to take into the heart and keep there every day that which should be fitted to strengthen faith, one feels how lightly and easily the word is taken away : it costs the devil little trouble.

Reader, if you are seeking Jesus, if you would come to faith, be admonished by this earnest word: "The devil comes and takes away the word, that they may not believe." Whatever temptation there may be, either from the world without or in your own heart, take heed that you always keep and hold fast the word. Let not the devil take it away from you. Let the precepts and promises of the word be your meditation day and night. "Let the word of Christ dwell in you richly" (Col. iii. 16). "Thy word have I laid up in mine heart. . . It is my meditation all the day" (Ps. cxix. 11, 97). This language of David must be yours; then, when you have found life, you will later on be able also to say with him: "This I have had, because I kept Thy precepts" (ver. 56). O soul, even the devil knows this : where the word dwells in the heart, there faith comes. Do you also learn this, and be assured that the humble, silent holding fast the living word of God will certainly be blessed to awaken faith in you also. God Himself has said that is the word, "which is able to save your souls" (Jas. i. 21); and as the word is received and kept in this hope, He is faithful to bestow by the Spirit the blessing of the word.

Before that word, the evil one retreats, as before the "It is written" out of Jesus' mouth: with and by that word, the Lord God and His Spirit come to the soul.

CHAPTER XXXI

The Gift of Faith

"To you it hath been granted in the behalf of Chris
. . . to believe in Him."—PHIL. i. 29.

FAITH a gift of God: this truth has been to
many a one the cause of fear and dread.
And yet this ought not to be. It rather yields
reasons for gladness and hope. It is always an
entirely perverse amplification of this statement
to say: "It is a gift, and thus I do not know
whether I shall ever receive it; if it were to be
found by personal effort, and if I had to call it
into existence by my own power, I should then
indeed take heed that I did not remain without
faith." Thus many a one reasons. No: the
reverse is the truth. If you could believe of
yourselves, by personal effort and work, you
would never do it, you should certainly be lost.
But since faith is given to us, since there is a
Lord in heaven who will implant and cherish
and care for that faith in us, then there is hope

that we may obtain and preserve that faith.   It
is a word of joyful hope.

And what makes the encouragement of this
word still greater — this faith is given *by
grace*.[1]   There is no question of worthiness or
merit, of wisdom or piety, of strength or dignity;
but it is given to the unworthy and the ungodly.
To those that do not seek Him, the sovereign
God comes with His drawing grace; through
the Spirit He works the conviction of sin and
of the need of His love; by His word He sets
Jesus before the soul as His gift to the sinner,
desirable and suitable, freely offered and acceptable, until the soul, under the hidden and indeed
effectual working of the Spirit, takes confidence
to appropriate the Saviour entirely to itself.
Yea, from beginning to end, along the whole
way, in the midst of continual sinfulness and
unfaithfulness on your part, it is *of grace given
to you* to believe in Him.

And that faith comes under the use of means
does not make it any the less *a gift*.   Of well-
nigh every gift of God one can be partaker only
by work.   We get bread in the sweat of our
brow, and yet we pray: "Give us this day our
daily bread."   We enjoy health through the use
of food and other means, and yet we always

[1] So Dutch Version, *in loc.*

thank the Lord for preserving us from sickness and death. No: the appointment of means only shows us how loving the gift is, how the Lord will move and open the spirit of man by its own activity to appropriate entirely for himself what his God will bestow upon him. This thought of our text does not deter from means, but gives the right desire and the right spirit to use them. The soul learns to understand that the Lord who gives it the word will also give the faith to receive it; that He who has given the promise will also bestow the fulfilment, although you feel that you cannot do it. Set yourself to believe, in the joyful confidence: *it is given.*

Reader, it is given by grace to believe in Jesus. Ask this grace humbly from the Lord, wait for it at His hands in a childlike spirit. Let every experience of failure, of unbelieving, of insensibility convince you, how unfortunate it would be if you had to believe of yourself, and how blessed it is that you may look to God for it. Keep yourself occupied with the word of promise, look to Jesus as appointed for you by God, in order that you may believe in Him; and in every endeavour to appropriate Him, and the promises of grace, work in silent gladness, inspired by the word: "It is granted unto you to believe in Jesus." The God who has had Jesus offered to me, who has awakened in me the first desire for Him, *will also give grace to believe.* In that blessed confidence I shall go forward, until secretly and gradually faith becomes living and visible. Yes, thank God, "it is granted to believe in Him.